The Self-Love Portrait

Feed Your Soul. Find Connection. Rediscover Yourself.

Amber Dawes

Table of Contents

About the Author

I know just how important self-love is because it is the tool that has allowed me to build a new life, one outside of the dark place I've pulled myself from.

In the past, I have been depressed, lonely, isolated, and unable to get out of the black hole I created. I felt a dissociation within myself for many years, but I have been able to come out the other end. I spent years struggling to understand the world we live in, but one thing I've always been passionate about is self-improvement. I turned my life around, and now I have the power to love life and its miraculous surprises!

I believe the power of self-love is within all of us. If you're feeling lost and overwhelmed, let me be the guiding light to a new path toward a more loving, accepting world! Join me on a risk-free journey of exploration as you uncover greater truths and establish an unwavering ability to love yourself.

Introduction

Do you feel lost in life? Have you been losing interest in things that used to excite you? Are you struggling with a sense of disconnection or having trouble finding purpose?

How different would your life look if you were able to fully love yourself?

Love, in its truest form, is self-love. The thing is, today's world doesn't make finding that kind of unique connection easy. From modern problems to age-old existential questions, many obstacles get in the way of our ability to love ourselves.

Chances are, you're searching for purpose and meaning in life, but it's not so clear what that looks like in the superficial, materialistic world we live in today. Cultivating self-love is the ultimate way to take back your power and alleviate the pressures of modern-day demands. Self-love can give you the strength to seize opportunities with your newfound confidence and handle life's challenges with ease!

Imagine waking up tomorrow with confidence that you will make it through your daily tasks with ease. What amazing things could you accomplish if you shed self-doubt and hesitation? Discover the art of self-love and realize your fullest potential!

In this book, the chapters ahead will help you paint the portrait of what it means to love yourself. This happens in 15 steps:

1. Accept that you are in control.

2. Take initiative for positive change.

3. Envision who you want to be.

4. Trust that you are capable of becoming that person.

5. Shed the picture society has created of you.

6. Befriend yourself.

7. Tap into what you *really* want.

8. Believe that you can get what you want.

9. Treat yourself with respect.

10. Immerse yourself in this social world around you.

11. Use the beauty of the now as motivation.

12. Let go of the past and rejuvenate your life.

13. Take the plunge and feel love fully.

14. Restore order in your life.

15. Continue to live authentically.

These next steps will be broken down with actionable advice and a welcoming perspective that can shift your way of thinking, leading you down new paths with endless doors of opportunity.

Embrace this change, and don't be afraid to nurture a new perspective. As you lay the stepping stones to the future ahead, you will gift yourself an unbreakable foundation for long-lasting change.

Self-love may feel uncomfortable at first, especially after years of neglecting this practice. However, by embracing these next steps, you'll discover the tools needed to build a unique portrait of what self-love looks like in your life.

Chapter 1:

Take Back the Driver's Seat

The average person dreams about two hours each night, even those who don't remember their dreams (Summer, 2024). During this time, our brains cycle through our experiences throughout the day, processing information and deciding what to store and what can be forgotten.

One common dream you may have experienced before is a scenario where you were in a moving car, unable to control where the vehicle goes. Perhaps the driver's seat is empty, someone else is driving, or maybe you are the driver but don't have control over where the car is going.

This concept can help us better understand what it means to feel like we are not the ones in control of our lives. It's a scary feeling, and even though we aren't the ones driving, it's hard to enjoy the view when you're constantly worried about what is going to come next.

You are the controller of your life, and though it can seem complicated and scary to take back that control, it is something entirely within your power. When you fail to take control over your life, you become a passenger, unable to change directions and stuck with what you have.

Now is the time to take back the driver's seat and turn the car in whichever direction you want to go on the road of your life.

This Is Your Story

When you ride through life as simply a passenger, you don't choose which direction to turn or what way to go. As time passes, you sit back, watching everything move around you while you sit in the passenger seat, not having any control over what happens next. On one hand, this is an easy way to move through life as you don't have to take responsibility for turning down the wrong direction. You avoid having to deal with the more challenging obstacles along the bumpy road.

However, when you have no control as a passenger, you're also stuck looking at whatever happens to be outside your window.

In life, if you're unhappy, uninspired, and even in a place where you dislike your surroundings, then it leaves you feeling drained. It becomes hard to find motivation to do the things you actually want to do, and negative perspectives on your surroundings may contribute to even more unhappy thoughts, thus creating a cycle of misery that chips away at you each time the cycle starts again.

When we fail to take control, we let someone else write our story. We sit back and watch life happen in front of us, feeling as though change is impossible. This contributes to feelings of hopelessness, as we are stuck wishing on something that doesn't carry any certainty. There will always be things outside of our control, and many things contribute to our story that we couldn't have predicted, but there are still many ways in which we can write the script of our lives.

This script dictates how we view our lives. Consider the difference between two movies that have similar plots. For example, one movie about a family moving into a new house may have a silly, light-hearted energy, whereas another might be a thriller movie about the family's experience in the new neighborhood. Similar stories have different scripts that change the way the story is told.

Perhaps you don't have control over the plot, but now, it's up to you to change what you can in your story. Write your own script.

How we view our lives determines how we act. If you struggle to find purpose and experience a lack of fulfillment, then it will be difficult to find the push you need to get through the day, take risks, and work hard for change.

Self-love and compassion are vital tools in the creation of the life you want. There are likely things you did have control over in the past that you failed to change, and maybe you knowingly made bad choices that had negative results. It can be hard to view things with a fresh perspective if you're still stuck wishing you could change the past.

Self-love allows us to see ourselves as human. Mistakes are a part of life. Bad decisions make us human. We all have regrets and wish we could've done things differently, but these regrets aren't the tools that will help you get to where you want to be. Now, it's time to embrace the past and let it help you write the story of who you are going to become in the future.

Self-love is not superficial. It's not just about appreciating what's on the outside, but instead, finding the beauty in your *whole story*. It can be hard to accept our life's story as our own when we are struggling with past regrets and difficult emotions. As we try to avoid undesirable situations, we move away from some of the most pivotal things that write our stories.

Every Past Moment

When you love someone, you love both their good and bad sides. Consider someone in your life now. One of your best friends surely has something flawed about them. Perhaps they aren't very good at communicating and don't respond to texts or phone calls as often as they should. Maybe they have a problem with forgetfulness and cancel plans at the last minute. Perhaps they like something that you don't like, or they don't like something that you love.

Consider your kids or pets. We love them unconditionally and don't care about their flaws. Your children, if you have any, have likely caused some chaos around the house. Maybe they stained your favorite shirt or drew all over the walls with a marker. Perhaps your dog ripped up your favorite pillow, or your cat scratched up your couch.

There are an endless amount of flaws, shortcomings, or other small quirks among the people that we love the most. But for them, we are often much more forgiving than we are of ourselves.

We forgive those we love because we understand that people are humans, and we don't hold them to such a high regard that we might hold ourselves to. Loving yourself means loving every single part of you—the good and the bad. This also means accepting the past and moving on to the future, knowing that the past doesn't have to define you.

If somebody in your life made a mistake in the past, unless it was something really big, you likely don't think about it as often as you think about your own mistakes. When we look back on our own mistakes, we are often cycling through what we could have or should have done. We're looking at all the scenarios in which we could have made a change, said something different, or done something differently to have a result that we feel more comfortable with.

What we may not realize in this moment of rumination is that we're looking for a form of control. We're trying to control our feelings of guilt, regret, or embarrassment because we no longer want to feel that emotion. The thing is, we are taking the wrong steps to try and control those emotions. Rather than just embracing our humanity and accepting that sometimes we make mistakes, we go back over the past and try to find ways that things were different or could have been different as a means to comfort ourselves at the moment.

Self-deprecation or self-blame can become so normalized that it's almost our coping mechanism for feeling regret over the past. We can't control the past, but hindsight does make us feel like we have power because then we can learn what *not* to do in the future. But sometimes that hindsight goes too far and we end up getting stuck in a mindset where we feel bad about everything.

The thing is, rumination like this can keep us trapped in the same mentality. Rumination is different from reflection in that there's usually no better outcome with rumination, and instead, we end up making ourselves feel even worse. Reflection is more restricted, and there are boundaries in reflection. Reflection helps us change and grow, and rumination keeps us in the same mindset, prone to making the same mistakes.

It's okay to look back on a past mistake and see what you could have done differently, but then it's time to move on. When we keep going back over the same thing, cycling through different scenarios, we sometimes get so lost in trying to remember or change the past that we confuse small details. When excessively ruminating, over time, we don't even remember what actually happened in the real scenario, and instead, are just fueling more feelings of anxiety.

Self-love means recalling past moments and looking at them fondly or, when needed, viewing them with a sense of change in mind and then moving on.

Rather than trying to go back and change the past, we have to learn how to embrace everything that we've been through as a part of our story.

Connect the pieces between what is good in your life and what you had to do on the journey to get there.

One example that can easily help us understand the concept of embracing the past is anybody who might have children. Perhaps you had kids when you were just a teenager, and you felt, at the time, this derailed the path of your life that you thought you were going to go down. Maybe you found yourself in an unfortunate scenario and had to leave a bad relationship after having kids with someone. While we might have endured unfortunate circumstances to get there, at the end of the day, we love our children and wouldn't change our story because we wouldn't want to risk not having the same wonderful children that we do.

Our story has been written by circumstances both in and out of our control, but now, it's time for us to look back on all the stepping stones that it took to get there and appreciate the intricacy of how every moment in our lives intertwines.

Small coincidences, life lessons, and unique interactions have helped us cultivate the mindset that we have now. We can embrace our past and realize that these experiences are tools that will help us build our future.

Find appreciation in how the small change of events has led you right to this moment, exactly where you are. Appreciate the uniqueness and absurdity of life, as this is the first step in wholeheartedly accepting yourself.

One practical application of embracing the past is by connecting to your shadow. Shadow work is the art of integrating the hidden parts of yourself from the past into the person you are today. This might be repressed feelings, neglected emotions, or stifled passions.

Shadow work often relates to healing your inner child as well. Much of our shadow becomes suppressed in the formative years of our life. This might mean neglecting a passion you had because you were made to feel as though it wasn't important in your home life. It could mean hiding a part of your identity because you aren't accepted in your community.

Acknowledge the shadow that has been following you around and look at your past in a refreshed way. This will enable you to reconnect with the deepest form of yourself. When you identify this vulnerable individual, it becomes easier to give them unconditional love, just as you would anyone else in your life.

Integrate Difficult Emotions

One of the most human things about us is our emotions. How we feel, react, and show these emotions is a unique human feature. While all animals experience fear, excitement, and more, humans have a complex set of behaviors and communication styles that differentiate them from other species.

Emotions are neither positive nor negative—feelings of all kinds are a normal part of the human experience. However, many of us may fear experiencing certain kinds of emotions because they make us feel good or bad. For example, having anxious thoughts about an upcoming event can be undesirable. We all know it never feels good to have anger at a friend or family member.

These emotions make us who we are. They tap into something deep within our nature and can tell us something greater about ourselves. Emotions are biological. Different feelings, thoughts, and behaviors can have an impact on our body's chemistry. For example, if you're having money problems, it may make you feel stressed consistently, disrupting your body's natural hormonal balance.

Taking control of our lives helps us regulate how we react to different feelings and emotions, thus granting us the power to have a positive impact on how we feel. Integrate difficult emotions as a means of embracing all parts of yourself.

Anger is a response. Fear is telling us something deeper. Boredom is a natural part of life. Don't shy away from these difficult emotions; embrace them. They are a part of who you are. It's not your fault that you've been through certain things or that you experience difficult emotions, but now it's within your control to use these emotions and respond to them appropriately.

Sometimes, happiness is confused as the act of being devoid of negative emotions. In reality, it's the opposite. Happy people can still experience negative feelings and challenging scenarios. The difference is that they may have the tools needed to cope with those feelings in effective and productive ways.

As you develop self-love, you will find out what it means to unconditionally love yourself. When we avoid the negative or let it define our story, acting with fear may come naturally, but showing yourself love will empower you more than you can imagine.

Choose Love Over Fear

Fear is powerful, but so is love. Fear can be one of the most influential emotions that we have because so much of our body is built around keeping us safe and protected.

Deep inside all of us is a stress response. This is how we react to threats, perceived issues, and other dangers around us.

For example, consider the last time you were outside alone late at night. Maybe you had to walk to your car after a late shift at work, or perhaps you were walking home after a night out with friends. As you walked down the quiet street and heard nothing but the wind blowing, you might have felt a little creep pass over your body. Maybe you noticed somebody in the distance or felt as though somebody was watching you. Perhaps you were worried that another person on the street was following you, or you were afraid of someone popping out of the alley or the bushes as you walked down the street. During these times of potential danger, we often feel a little fear in our bodies. It's not that you're running down the street panicked. You're just a little more aware than you would be if it was the middle of the day and the street was bustling with people.

This fear response serves as a means to keep you protected. When you are on alert in that way, you're more prepared to deal with any potential threats. If somebody was waiting for you in the alley, then you might be able to cross the street and call for help, versus getting caught off guard by somebody surprising you randomly.

The fear response is what tells us to reach out for help. If we feel like we're slipping and falling, we reach for a railing. The fear response will make us question if we should seek help for any excessive pain we're feeling or symptoms of illness coming over us. The fear response keeps us working hard at our jobs so that we make enough money to pay our bills. Unfortunately, the fear response can go a little too far and have us feeling intense emotions like panic or anxiety over things that aren't actually that bad and in times when we are actually safe.

For example, consider the last time you were at a social event and felt a little awkward. Maybe after the event was done and you got home for the day, you felt worried about some of the things you said. You ruminated on the situation, and you can't help but think about embarrassing moments that you had, regretting certain social interactions and wishing that you'd done things differently. It's good to have some social awareness and to reflect on interaction so that you can improve your social and communication skills—however, you shouldn't beat yourself up about it, and for the most part, we often get stuck on things that aren't even that big of a deal. Chances are, the other individual doesn't even remember the things that you said, even though you might be replaying the same situation over and over again in your mind. The fear response is good for keeping us alive, but sometimes, it can be something that keeps us stuck in an unproductive mindset.

Fear can keep us from taking risks. It keeps us from interacting and meeting new people. Fear keeps us missing out on opportunities. Intuition is important, and it's helpful to ensure you make the right choices in life. But what's more important is acting with love.

Choose love over fear. When you tell yourself, "I did something really embarrassing yesterday," respond to that fear with love. Say, "I am human, and even if I did make a mistake, others still love me."

Every time you have that sense of panic creeping inside of you, it's easy to react with fear of the unknown. Fear has many faces, like anger, jealousy, and a need for control. Sometimes, we may fear the parts of ourselves that we don't understand. We may fear other people, especially those who are different from us. Fear might be the first instinct you feel, but replace that with love and a desire to learn more and connect.

Make choices to understand deeper rather than shying away from fear.

Fear and love can be similar. Sometimes, the more we love someone, the more we fear for their safety or their happiness. Sometimes, when we look at ourselves, we fear ourselves. We think that there's something wrong with us, that we're not able to find success, or we believe that we are inherently broken because we keep making the same mistakes over and over again. Overload yourself with love during these vulnerable times! It's what you need to be kind to yourself and work through the intense emotions you're experiencing.

You might be fearful of your future and your own intentions. You might question whether or not you're a good person and if you're doing the right things. You fear that you're not doing enough or that you're too different from others. The fears that you have around yourself can be turned into love that impassions you. Remember that you are human. Give yourself compassion, and let yourself feel connected to the world around you.

Fear may make us wary of others. We think their intentions might be negative or that they are more judgmental than they actually are. Trust in yourself and trust others until they give you a valid reason not to. Don't listen to the biggest fears in your mind, or else they will drive your life. When we follow fear, we are led astray, and it can be hard to go back through damaged paths.

If you travel through this upcoming journey with fear over the idea of loving yourself, it can manifest in many ways. You might create hesitation around the idea of self-love, creating resistance on your journey. Two strategies can help you overcome these obstacles: believing that you are capable of change and striking a balance between positive and negative emotions.

Believe That You're Capable

Believe that you can make positive changes and that you are capable of loving yourself, or else it will feel nearly impossible to do so. Things won't get better on their own—you have to make it happen, but to get the ball rolling, you have to believe you're capable in the first place.

To realistically change and actually see a difference, we need to have the patience to allow ourselves to heal and grow.

Self-love isn't a switch—it's a practice that gradually grows over time. Each experience you have is one that can contribute to your knowledge and skills needed to strengthen self-love. Even when conflict approaches and you're not sure how to move on, remember that you will get through this. You will overcome the challenges, and even if bad things happen, you'll have what it takes to make this a learning lesson.

Take some time to reflect on something about you that has changed over time for the better. Did you grow out of old habits? Did you work hard to practice saving money and start investing in your future? Did you find someone you love, and you've started a family? Identify

14

something good that has happened and use this moment as a reminder that you *are* capable and positive change *is* coming your way.

If you don't believe, then as you are on the cusp of change, you will automatically give up. It will feel natural to make excuses to keep things the way they are. Taking steps for positive change is important, but beyond this, you have to accept that you are capable of fully loving yourself, or else it'll be a hard goal to follow.

Managing the Negative and Positive

You control your experience, so you control the perspective you have. You have the power to see both the positive and negative, and this will give you the knowledge to focus on what is necessary to make great things happen in your life.

Start to notice negativity in yourself and others. Negativity is natural, and you're not a bad person, or there's nothing inherently wrong with you if you have negative thoughts.

However, we have to recognize that there's a decision we make when we are negative. The decision is that we are continuing to perpetuate that mindset. You might have a negative reaction to a scenario around you, such as anger or frustration. It's up to you to notice that negativity and find a solution or to keep festering with that negativity, allowing it to grow on its own. It's a hard decision to control, but it is one that we can slowly change over time. You may still choose negativity 9/10 times, but with each choice you make, you will grow closer to leading with positivity.

This is a way to help you notice how we might be able to start controlling the script of our lives. For example, are you someone who complains often? Do you give off negative energy to others, or are you more welcoming and open? The energy that you put out into the world is the energy that you'll experience back. The more positivity and love you put out in the world, the more your world changes around you. Start noticing these small differences, because that will help you raise awareness of the way that you're thinking and acting. This first stage of self-love is all about building awareness. Right now, you're living through each day, likely unaware of just how much you're contributing to a negative mindset. Start the process of raising awareness over your emotions, as this will help you improve your ability to practice self-love.

In Summary

Failing to take control can become a comfort, as that means giving responsibility to outside circumstances.

- You are in control of your life, no matter what things you've experienced so far.

- Every past moment you've lived through is one that helps define who you are.

- Embrace these moments with appreciation and fondness and it will be easier to cope.

- Don't shy away from difficult emotions and experiences; they are lessons that can help you understand yourself.

- Choose love over fear, as this will help you manage fearful emotions in the process.

- Believe that you're capable of making change, or else it will be difficult to integrate change into your life.

- Raise awareness over the negativity you're putting out in the world to have more control over the positivity you receive.

Self-love starts when we choose to love ourselves. We may *want* to love ourselves, but *deciding* to live in that fashion is different. Know this difference and get in the driver's seat of your life to head in the direction of the change you desire.

Chapter 2:

Be the Maker of Your Own Destiny

It only takes a second to change the course of your life forever. Sometimes, the most influential moments we experience are split seconds, but the fallout lasts a lifetime. Each day brings 86,400 seconds, meaning there are tens of thousands of chances to change the direction of our life's journey.

When we fail to take control, that could mean giving away thousands of chances for change each day. We let people we hate, things we don't like, and repeated patterns make decisions for us all day long. For instance, think about the last time you saw something you didn't like. Maybe it was a post from someone on social media, or perhaps it was a bad TV show. How long did this bother you? When feelings like anger, annoyance, frustration, and other unfavorable emotions take control, we're giving up our power and letting negative influences take the steering wheel.

It's not always easy to let go of emotions, especially for triggering circumstances. However, repeating the practice of taking control is our responsibility. Wanting change and making change are two different things, and the idea of overnight success is a myth. Small habits build. You're the bricklayer of the structure of your life.

Don't let others play the main role in your life. Don't let outside circumstances define you. Don't let the past prevent you from building something great.

Follow your own blueprint and build the life you want.

Your Responsibility

You are responsible for your life, and your life only. That includes the way that you react to the things you've been given that were out of your control, which can be the challenging part of your responsibility. You might not have been able to help it if you were born into a certain position, but you are now capable of changing how you handle your current situation.

The problem with taking responsibility is that people often confuse what is in and what is out of their control. This is followed by a tendency to try and change what's not within your control and neglect what you could change.

One big factor that's often not thought of as something that's within your control is your emotions. Emotions, however, are complex. Every emotion has a trigger, a response, and then a reaction. The trigger is the inciting incident, which could be a major event or a simple thought. What follows is an emotional response, usually based on your feelings, such as anger or happiness. Lastly is your reaction. The reaction is how that feeling is handled.

For example, picture three drivers on the road: Bob, Stacy, and Nick. Nick is speeding and cuts them both off. Both Bob and Stacy just experienced a similar situation to each other, which acts as the trigger, followed by an emotional response. Stacy is scared and worried about this dangerous driver, whereas Bob is angered and feels offended that he was cut off. Next is a reaction to that feeling. Stacy slows down to stay far away from the dangerous driver, whereas Bob speeds up, wanting to get a look at the offender. As you can see, both their emotional responses and reactions can differ.

Every driver on that road can have a different combination of responses and reactions after experiencing the triggering scenario. In this example, the trigger is out of everyone's control. They couldn't help that the other driver cut them off, but the reaction was within their control.

Many people fail to take full responsibility in their lives because they are unaware that there is a difference between our response and our reaction. You'll hear this often. People will say things like, "I couldn't help it; I was mad," in response to their behavior.

For the most part, we can't help our emotional response, but we can help how we react to that. Often, the more intense an emotion, the more difficult it is to control your reaction, but it is still within your control.

Our emotional responses are often learned and developed over life. Some people are very outwardly emotional and feel things intensely, whereas others have a tendency to withdraw or suppress emotion. In the present, you can't help your emotional response for the most part, yet you can learn to change it with time.

What is something that bothers you, no matter how hard you try to let it go? Now, it's your responsibility to notice the trigger, response, and reaction of this inciting incident. The first step is raising awareness of the trigger and your emotions. Then, with time, learn to change your reaction. As you keep practicing this, eventually, you'll reduce the intensity of your emotional response as well.

Other people can trigger you, hurt you, and try to break you down, but you always have control over how you react to that. Let yourself feel the emotion fully, but know where your responsibility lies to maintain control in your life.

Show yourself love, grace, and compassion when reacting, and make decisions from a place where your best interest is in mind.

Make Decisions

Be a decision-maker, have initiative, and be proactive. Think of this as the DIP method:

- decisiveness

- initiative

- proactivity

Failing to take action in your life is a failure to take control. That control is then given to others, meaning it becomes harder for you to make changes in your life. Decisions are hard to make. It essentially feels like we're pressing a button to transport us to a specific future. Juxtaposing that to an alternate reality makes even the smallest choices feel like heavy burdens. But to love yourself deeply means trusting yourself to make the right decisions. Practice decisiveness because failing to make a decision is a decision in itself. There's no escaping the decision-making process, so you may as well choose so you have the awareness and presence needed to appreciate the good decisions and learn from the bad ones.

Have the initiative to know what decisions need to be made in the first place. Be willing to stand up, speak up, and act accordingly. Use the voice you've been given and take a plunge into the unknown. When you learn to embrace every one of life's lessons, no experience will ever be a waste or a regret. Be a go-getter and take the first step in your endeavors. Take each moment as it passes and maximize your experiences by embracing all parts of them. Having initiative will empower you in all areas of life.

Be a decision-maker and do what you can to be proactive so that things go the way you want them to. Making a decision is an important step, but then you need to act out those next steps to get to the outcome. Saying you're going to do something is different than doing it. After trying one thing or taking the first step, do it again, and again, and again. Repeat behavior to make changes, and have the patience needed to help yourself cope through the process. Being proactive helps amplify your decisiveness and initiative.

DIP into a pool of risks, opportunities, and chances. Accept making the wrong decisions, and know your choices might not turn out the way you hope. This increases your humanity as you embrace the art of not knowing it all. It will lighten your load and make it easier for you to wholeheartedly love yourself. Let go of your humility and get excited about the idea of experimenting and exploring life.

Decisions aren't just about picking between two options. Decisions define who we are and how we interact in the world. We decide what we like, what to say to others, and what to eat for dinner. We decide what to listen to, what to read, and what to believe. Make a choice and stand by it. Sometimes, you may find that you learn something new or experience a situation that changes your beliefs, and that's okay. You will, and should, shift perspectives with time.

Shift Perspectives

Self-love fuels self-growth, and self-growth is all about embracing the learning process. Accept new ideas into your life, and be okay with shifting perspectives. Conviction is important, and you should have things you believe in. However, those beliefs look different as time passes. You learn new things with age and experiences, and it's okay not to have the same outlook as you used to. Our core values are generally the same, but it doesn't make your beliefs any less authentic if you shift perspective over time. In fact, it's the opposite. The process of shifting perspectives is one that challenges current beliefs, strengthening those core values as you reflect on them and question their veracity. Embrace the idea that your mind *can* change, and it will change.

What kind of perspectives are important to shift? One main one to focus on is to be less judgy and don't be quick to criticize others.

You only know what is going on in your life, meaning you don't know what's going on in someone else's that might be causing them to act a certain way. When you judge someone's life, you're putting your own situation into theirs. You're assuming you would act a certain way and make certain choices. But you're only able to have that mindset because of the unique and specific set of scenarios you've lived through.

Judgments about others can come back to bite us when we start making those same harsh judgments against our lives and situations. When you view someone else's situation from your own perspective, then you end up viewing someone else's successes from your own perspective as well. However, some people have different lives and opportunities than you, so it's unfair to make these comparisons.

You create the meters and spectrums you live on in terms of judgments against others. Society has beauty standards, but you can create your own. There are tests to measure intelligence, but what looks smart to someone might not look the same to someone else. We can only decide how to judge others based on our own experiences, which is often unfair to the whole truth of the scenario.

When you stop judging others so harshly, you lighten up on yourself, thus allowing more room for self-love.

Take Accountability

Acknowledging your responsibilities is an important step, but accountability means consistently owning up to that, whether it's making up for past mistakes or goals you are setting for the future. Stay true to your word, and learn to trust yourself. Accountability is what comes after proactivity. Are you sticking by what you said? Are you correcting mistakes you've made? Are you recognizing what needs to change and then keeping up with that change?

If you always let yourself down, it can be hard to trust yourself, and love is heavily dependent on trust. To love someone means you believe in their good intentions and you accept all parts of them.

Growing and becoming a better version of yourself can be challenging for those who fail to take accountability. As humans, we all know deep down we are inherently flawed. We might make bad decisions or hurt people—intentionally and unintentionally. Sometimes, that can lead to self-deprecation. However, accountability goes deeper than that. It's easy to say, *I'm sorry, I messed up.* What's hard is saying what the specific mistake was and what steps are going to be taken to ensure those mistakes don't happen again. Many people will say sorry but fail to own up to what they're actually sorry about.

Acknowledge the impact of decisions as well as the lasting impact that failing to take responsibility has had. Own up to these mistakes, and let yourself fully feel guilt and regret. Then, make it your responsibility to move on. Remember, regret and guilt will not take us far. The next part of forgiving yourself is challenging because that means fully acknowledging the things we did that we felt were wrong. Once you can admit specific mistakes and what steps you're taking next, you can finally forgive yourself and see the past in a new way. Rather than trying to change what can't be changed, you can finally free yourself to take the next steps to a happier, healthier, and more wholesome life.

Let Go of Guilt

Once you start recognizing the things that are actually within your control, it then becomes easier to let go of guilt for the things no longer in your control. Sometimes, guilt is also a result of a failure to take accountability. When you own up to what you did that you wish you could change, you find solutions for preventing it from happening again and making amends if possible. This helps you become more forward-focused rather than wanting to go to the past and make changes.

Guilt is a reaction to experiencing something unfortunate. The thing is, sometimes, guilt isn't doing anything but hurting us. For example, let's say you have guilt over how you treated someone in the past. Perhaps in junior high, you were mean to another classmate. Your guilt doesn't undo the hurt they might've felt. There's a chance they are no longer affected by this past experience anyway. However, that repeated guilt might make you feel bad about yourself in the present. You use it to believe you are inherently flawed. You convince yourself you ruined this person's life, but in reality, you're only hurting yours over and over.

We can hold onto our regrets as learning opportunities, but we need to let our feelings around them dissipate. Let guilt transform into a mental note rather than a repeated act of harm against your mind and body.

Guilt isn't something to feel ashamed of having—it's a sign you are capable of remorse. This is a good thing because it means you have empathy and compassion and actually care about other people. However, repeated guilt can lead to excessive regret, which further harms you.

23

Walk the high road and don't look back. Guilt can sometimes be our attempt to change the past. If we keep going over and over a scenario in our head, maybe we'll find a way to change things or see things differently. Rather than trying to change the past, use guilt as a reminder that you are simply a human experiencing emotions. Learn from what you can use bits to help you move forward, and let go of the rest.

Stop Silent Competitions

On the other side of the spectrum of emotion, the opposite of guilt is jealousy. Feeling bad for someone is one emotion, but being envious of someone is much different. However, both can equally impede our ability to move on and grow for the better. Most competitions happen in our heads. Even when there is a somewhat mutual competition going on between you and another person, it might never be spoken aloud. For example, if you're fighting against a coworker for a promotion, you may go the duration without discussing this with one another. If you feel sibling rivalry, it might be an unspoken competition that spans years.

Whenever we get lost in a competitive mindset with someone else, we end up making them our focal point. Rather than focusing on how we can love ourselves and be the best version of ourselves possible, we focus on how we can be better than them. We may even have the desire to "take them down," resulting in a heightened emotional state.

You are not in competition with anyone. Think of it as if you were a runner in an upcoming marathon; you are only in competition with the last version of yourself that competed. Push yourself to get a faster running time; don't make the focal point that you want to beat everyone. A runner who is running for themselves sees the finish line, putting all of their energy into reaching that point. Someone highly competitive might be looking around at others too much, distracted from the end goal, and slowing down as they let thoughts of insecurity flood their head.

Focus on yourself and improve by taking small steps forward with your personal goals in mind. Think of it as showing up to cheer yourself on.

Rather than fixating on winning a competition, be your own cheerleader on the sideline who only cares about you doing your best.

Letting go of a competitive nature helps you see others as fellow humans rather than enemies. Instead of focusing on how to be better or prove yourself, you can embrace them as whole humans, thus improving your connections in the process.

Stop assuming the worst about others, and give them grace. Notice how you might be judging others unconsciously. For example, if you go to a social event and chat with another person, you might leave feeling embarrassed about something you said. Maybe you said something silly or made a joke no one laughed at. It's normal to feel a little insecure, but you might find yourself spiraling into intense rumination over this social quip. Maybe you keep thinking about how this other person is probably judging you or making assumptions about who you are.

This belief that someone might be negatively thinking about you isn't a judgment against you; instead, it's actually *you* judging *them*. You're assuming the worst—that they're judgmental, making fun of you, and believing bad things about you. In reality, they are probably focused on their own social quips and are remembering your conversations fondly. Other people are kinder and more compassionate than they may seem. We can all connect to each other on humanness and the self-belief patterns we may share.

Ditch the gossip because when you change how you talk about others, you change how you talk about yourself. Next time you find yourself gossiping, imagine someone else talking about you in the way you're talking about them. It doesn't feel very good and serves as a reminder that the people we're talking about are humans just like us. Also, you can assume that those willing to gossip *with* you might also be gossiping *about* you.

Comparison is a trap because you will always be able to compare more things, big and small, leaving you always dissatisfied and longing for more. Chances are you also often compare your worst to someone else's best. You only see bits and pieces of everyone's life, but you see the whole picture from your own perspective.

The magic of theater looks different to the audience than it does to the director behind the scenes. People show you a version of what they want you to see, and you formulate opinions based on your unique perspective. Trying to make sense of it all is hard enough, not to mention the added layer of comparison in the mix.

Take practical steps to reduce your desire to compare yourself and stop self-sabotaging. Embrace everyone's uniqueness and focus on your journey. This will help you carve the path for the rest of what's left to be written about your story!

In Summary

Others may influence you, but it's important not to allow them to take control and remember that it's always *you* who is in charge. The world around us is competitive, intense, and judgmental, but we can decide for ourselves what to think and feel and then act accordingly.

- Know what is in and out of your control so you can take responsibility for the things in your life that you want to change.

- Be proactive and seek out the things you want in this life— remember, indecision is a decision.

- Shift your perspective and allow in a new way of thinking so you can further reinforce that change *is* possible and much deserved.

- Take accountability for your actions and own up to the things you want to change.

- Shed guilt and move away from this feeling so you can transform it into the power to change.

- Stop competing with others and embrace your own uniqueness to allow more self-love in your life.

Being the maker of your life is one of the most loving things you can do for yourself.

Chapter 3:

Mold Your Best Self

Choose yourself over and over again. Put the power of you into execution. Imagine the person you want to be, and then make the choice to be this person.

Nearly half of our habits occur without us even thinking about them (Palmer, 2020). They occur as we're watching TV or scrolling on our phones. When was the last time you didn't realize you'd finished a snack or drink? Have you ever completed a chore quickly as you talked to a housemate or listened to your favorite song? Often, we unconsciously go through routines or rituals without even realizing we're doing them.

This leads us to get lost in our habits and routines, failing to make changes to be a better version of ourselves.

Now, it's up to you to mold the version of the person you want to be. Uncover the person you know you are and who you truly want to be, and then decide to support them in whatever way possible. Embrace your imperfections because these can help build your identity and may serve as the very things you can use as a vessel for endless self-love.

Your Decision

The choice is yours: Will you keep repeating the same cycles, or are you ready to love yourself?

This decision comes in three parts: Decide to put yourself first in the love department, be kinder to your emotions, and decide who you are.

Don't let the thoughts of others drag you down or make you second-guess who you want to be. This is especially important to remember for those who want to be different than they are now. We don't like to change because if we fail at that change, others will see that failure. We don't want to be put under a microscope by those around us, so we can sometimes get stuck doing the same things, repeating the same behavior, all for the sake of avoiding judgment from others. However, deep down, we may be stifling parts of ourselves that we know we want to unleash.

If you are always living with feelings of disappointment and wanting to change, you will always repeat the same cycle. Be the person you want to be, and the change will follow. See yourself in a positive light, and it will act as a reminder to make improvements each day.

Know Your Priorities

First and foremost, you have to remember that you're human. Know your self-worth and protect the things that you deserve. You deserve to have your basic human rights fulfilled.

This includes rights such as having a home you enjoy, feeling safe, and spending time doing the things you love. You are equal to every other person on the planet, and you deserve the exact same things that everyone else deserves.

It's easier for us to have empathy for other people because of our inherent human nature. Humans want to help each other. Sure, there are bad people in the world, and you'll see many terrible things happen in your lifetime, whether you experience that firsthand or hear about it from others. But that doesn't mean that humans, in general, are bad. The news doesn't share stories about how friends help each other out. There aren't countless documentaries and podcasts about families that come together to support each other. Instead, you'll see countless extreme stories of violence, abuse, and neglect because journalists, podcast creators, and documentarians know that this gains more attention. More people are going to talk about a mother who mistreated her children than a mother who sacrificed everything to make sure that they got the things that they wanted.

Sometimes, we live in a world where there are so many bad things happening around us that it's easy to begin to think that the world is a bad place. We see and hear about so much tragedy that it can be hard to feel like humans are inherently good. We have to remember that humans, like all living things, are simply animals doing their best to survive along the way. Other people's bad decisions are not proof that the world is inherently a bad place.

We are not the ones who decide how someone gets to live. There is law and order in the world to help put regulations in place, which is a first attempt at organizing some of the chaos of life. But beyond that, an individual doesn't get to decide what someone deserves or doesn't deserve. This philosophy must apply to yourself.

Bad things happen, and bad people exist, but at the end of the day, that doesn't mean the world is bad. Humans are flawed, and you're included in this group of flawed individuals. Despite those flaws, you still deserve to have your basic human rights met.

As you start to embrace human nature and be more empathetic and accepting of the people around you, it becomes easier to start accepting who you are. You are equal to everyone else, and you deserve the same things as everyone else.

We have to have humility, we have to have empathy, we have to have understanding, and we have to treat everybody with the same kind of dignity that humans deserve. Now, it's time to apply all of those rules to yourself. You deserve to feel safe, you deserve to feel accepted, and you deserve to feel fulfilled. You deserve to protect your safety. You deserve to be who you are so that you can feel wholly accepted. You deserve to prioritize the things that make you happy and help you find fulfillment.

These basic human rights should become your priorities.

Sometimes, we create this internal punishment system where we might feel like we're not deserving of certain things or that we aren't good enough to have the things we want in our lives. Sometimes, this internal system becomes so ingrained in our psyche that we subconsciously begin punishing ourselves. We think we don't deserve to have our rights met because of our thoughts or actions, so we ultimately don't fulfill those basic needs.

Consider something like self-sabotage. No one wants to struggle and do things they regret, but often, it happens because we don't think we deserve a different life. Remember your priorities and what you deserve, which are your natural human rights.

Beyond this, we also have to remember that we still deserve to be happy. We deserve to find fulfillment. For this reason, remember not to chase after things that don't make you happy. If you do, what ends up happening is that you get stuck on a hamster wheel, always wishing things were different. If you follow somebody else's timeline for your life, you lose control. If you ignore your dreams because of somebody else's judgment, then you ignore yourself. You start creating a system where you neglect your own needs, thus failing to get the things that you deserve.

Focus on what matters most and forget everything else. Remember your priorities!

Start with your basic human needs. For example, this includes the right to eat and have proper nutrition. Consider somebody who's always struggled with their weight. They wish that they could lose weight. They want to be thinner than they are. They hate their body and are unhappy with their eating routine. Perhaps they start restricting food as a form of punishment. Maybe they tell themselves they're only allowed to eat food if they do something else first, like work out. But the problem with this is that food is not a reward; it's a human right.

We all deserve to eat. It's okay to want to alter what you eat in an attempt to have a healthier lifestyle, but you shouldn't restrict and withhold it as a form of punishment. This goes for all of our basic human needs, like sleeping or working out.

When we restrict ourselves or don't take the steps to meet these needs, this is not self-love. This is self-harm. In the example mentioned, it may be misconstrued as self-love because that person believes they're trying to take steps to become thinner, but they're not doing it healthily. Instead, they are damaging their relationship with food.

Know your priorities and take care of yourself as a human because this is how you will lay the groundwork for loving yourself.

Respect Your Own Boundaries

Once you've established your priorities and recognized your human rights, it's time to learn how to respect your own boundaries. That means, when you tell yourself, *I deserve to be happy*, you set boundaries to protect that happiness. When you tell yourself, *I deserve to be safe*, you set boundaries to make yourself feel safer. Know what to prioritize, and then put boundaries and rules in place to ensure you are able to maintain those priorities.

Stay true to yourself. Focus on yourself. Focus on your boundaries. You cannot control somebody else's emotions or actions. You can only control your own. This is why it's so crucial to set boundaries that protect you and to ensure that those protections stay in place.

Don't let other people's actions or even your own impulses cloud your judgment. Other people can be manipulative. They can be influential, and they can spark fear in you and make you second-guess yourself. Remember your priorities and what you want to get from this life and keep that protected.

Define self-love for yourself. What does that look like? That might mean putting a few hours aside each day to work on your passion. When somebody asks you to hang out or do something during these hours, then protecting your priorities would mean saying no because you're busy.

Self-love might mean changing career paths. When a family member tries to dissuade you from doing that and tells you you're making a bad decision, respecting your boundaries means telling them that you will keep doing what you want. You can thank them for their concern, but you can also share that you're focused on yourself and you're going to make decisions that are best for you.

Love is all about centering yourself and realizing that you should use the same compassion on yourself that you give to other people. Other people do not deserve the love that you have more than you do. You should come first, and once you learn how to love yourself and prioritize your boundaries, you'll then start to learn how you can share that love with other people.

Identify your values. These go beyond just our personal goals. These are the basic truths that we have for ourselves. On a more obvious level, values include practicing Christianity, Judaism, Hinduism, and other religions. Values are practicing veganism or being an environmentalist. But values go beyond these lifestyles. They are also about how we treat other people. This might mean having the value that you will not call other people names and that you'll stay calm and collected when you have conflict. Values mean making the right decision, even though it might not be easy.

Values mean protecting yourself and your boundaries, even if that means not being able to show up for them in the same way that you show up for yourself. Your boundaries shouldn't hurt others, but they also shouldn't cater to others. They should first prioritize you and what you need.

Identify your values, your boundaries, and your priorities. These help define the rules for how you will love yourself.

Identify the things that you want more than anything else. What do you need to do to protect that? What do you need to do to make sure that you respect yourself in the process?

Some of these concepts might be things that you already kind of know. For example, you know that you need to take care of yourself. You know that you need to live a healthy lifestyle. You know that you need to spend time relaxing and enjoying yourself.

But *knowing* and *believing* are two vastly different concepts.

You know that you deserve to be protected, but now you have to believe that you *deserve* to be protected. It's a feeling that goes deep within you, and it's something to learn how to build and cultivate. The biggest thing that might get in the way of this belief system is believing that you are defined by your worst imperfections. Rather than letting these imperfections hinder us from getting the things that we want, it's time to practice embracing these imperfections to connect us further to our humanity and accept that we are not always going to be perfect people.

Embrace Imperfections

Be authentically you, and boost your self-esteem by embracing imperfections. Know that these unique qualities are yours, and they deserve to be celebrated. Remember that others are as forgiving of our imperfections as we are of them.

Perfection doesn't exist, especially when it comes to emotions. You are human, and emotions are symbols and signals that are trying to tell you something deeper. Emotions are simply the first step in the process of understanding something deeper about ourselves.

You are born human and will always live as one, so accept these emotions now to become your own best friend. Treat your emotions the way you would anyone else, and let these imperfections flourish.

When we identify an imperfection, we have two choices:

- Forgive ourselves if it is a mistake we made or something out of our control.

- Accept what we can't change and learn to embrace it as a part of ourselves.

Learn the Art of Forgiving

Oftentimes, in our past, we make mistakes, and we do things that we wish we hadn't done. In the present, we might try to justify these actions and decisions rather than just accept them for what they are. Instead of saying *I was wrong*, we might try to look for the reasoning behind what we did. We try to justify those decisions and tell ourselves that it wasn't that bad. We try to downplay the situation, or maybe we even fill in the blanks with facts that we don't quite remember, simply for the sake of not having to admit that we are wrong.

Rather than trying to change the past or make excuses, it's essential that we learn how to simply embrace those imperfections and accept those mistakes. For example, maybe in the past, you got into some trouble with the law.

You tell yourself, *Oh, I was only 18. I didn't know any better*. Sure, everyone makes mistakes, and it's good to recognize that youth can lead us to make poor decisions. However, some people might try and justify what they did. They think to themselves, *Well, it's my parents' fault for not teaching me better,* or *I fell into the wrong crowd, and I was influenced poorly*.

If we don't take accountability for what we did, then we won't change. If we say, *Oh, it's my parent's fault*, then as an adult, we might still blame our parents for certain things. If we say, *I got caught up in the wrong crowd*, then we blame pure influence. What we really have to do is simply accept what we did. While sure, there may have been influences, it's okay to tell yourself, *I messed up, I made a mistake. I shouldn't have done that*. That's the most important first step in taking accountability.

Then after, take action, reflect, and learn from this mistake. Ask yourself, *What led me to make that decision?*

Did you want to fit in with the crowd? Did you have resentment that you needed to take out because of issues from your past or even issues with your parents? There was a force within you, not outside of you, that led you to make those decisions. Other people might have played a role. They might have pushed you in a certain direction, but no matter what happened, you still made those choices.

Taking accountability is taking back your power.

When we were younger, we didn't know better. We did make mistakes, and that's okay. That's a part of being young. Learn the art of forgiving. There's a difference between forgiving yourself and moving on and justifying your actions, which will only keep you stagnant. Imperfections are often stemming from two categories:

- things from our past that we wish we could change

- inherent characteristics that we were born with

If your imperfection is an inherent characteristic you were born with, then that requires acceptance. You can't change it. Maybe you don't like a facial feature you were born with. Perhaps you wish you were taller, shorter, wider, or thinner. Maybe you wish you had curly hair, but you have straight hair. Whatever it may be, you can't change these things. There are certain procedures you could try. You might consider plastic surgery to fix some of these imperfections—and that's okay if you do need to make changes. By all means, do what you need to do to feel comfortable and confident in yourself.

However, embracing these imperfections can make your life easier because sometimes, even when we make those changes, we still aren't happy with ourselves. Learn how to love yourself first. Then, if you still want to make small changes, go for it. But if you are dependent on these changes and on these alterations for your happiness, then it might never happen. You end up using way too many procedures to try and fill the void within you when, in reality, self-love is what is actually needed and what is going to fill that hole.

Aside from the imperfections that you were born with, sometimes, imperfections are a result of mistakes and decisions that we made in the past. For example, perhaps you dropped out of school, and now you don't have a high school degree. Maybe you're finding it difficult to find a job. Perhaps you chose to move away, and now you're unhappy with where you live, but you are stuck with a certain job and can't move again.

Maybe you made some poor financial decisions, and now you are in debt and not making enough money to get you out of debt. Whatever these perceived flaws or imperfections might be, moving on from them starts with forgiving yourself for the things that *were* within your control. Did you take out too many loans at a young age? Maybe once you turned 18, you took out 5 credit cards and a personal loan, and now, in your 40s, you're still paying these off because of the high interest rates. When we make choices in the past that we regret, it can be difficult to move on.

Forgive yourself for these things. Admit that you made a mistake, whatever it may be, and then move on. How would you talk to somebody else who made the same mistake?

Forgiveness lies within your grasp every single day. Forgiveness can be hard because sometimes we get stuck in a world outside reality. We try to think of how we could change things. Guilt can be an attempt to enact control. When you get stuck in a loop of rumination, you might think to yourself, *If only I had done this, or if only I had done that, things would be vastly different.* That may be true, but there's no going back in time. There's nothing we can do to make different decisions that have already been made.

This is where tough love needs to come in to help you move on. Tough love is your reality check back to the present moment, where you can feasibly find ways to not necessarily make changes but to move on and accept what has already happened.

If you are stuck in the past when it comes to something like excessive debt or not getting a high school degree, you can't go back in time. You can't undo taking out those loans, and you can't undo dropping out of high school. If you get stuck in this regret and guilt cycle, then you're stuck in the past. You're not actually making good decisions for the present but instead chasing after the dream that maybe you could change the past. Instead, you have to use tough love to give yourself that reality check that there's no going back. You have to accept that this is the situation. This is what you've been handed, even if it was you who handed this to yourself.

Forgiveness means accepting that you can't make a change and what has happened has happened.

Forgiveness is the promise that you're going to move on, prioritize your needs, and remember that it is possible to make good decisions for the future. You can make changes for the days ahead, and you can use your past experiences to help you move on and live a different life. Move on to a life anew by practicing the art of forgiveness and learning how to let go so you can live happily, once again.

Master the Act of Acceptance

In case you have trouble remembering—you are enough! Another part of embracing imperfections is accepting what cannot be changed.

This starts with the things about ourselves that we were born with. As mentioned previously, you cannot make those changes. You can make small alterations, but there are certain things that we have to learn how to accept and embrace as being part of who we are.

On a deeper level, we have to not only accept ourselves but master the art of *embracing* ourselves, and this means that our worst criticisms are not true. The worst things you believe about yourself do not define who you are. Often, we become our own biggest bullies, and it can be hard to avoid that mindset because, for so long, we've believed that our bullies are true and that everything they say is right.

That is not the case! Don't take criticism to heart. Sometimes, when we take criticism, it almost validates all the things that we believe about ourselves.

For example, picture a young college student who is the ultimate perfectionist. They believe that anything less than an A+ is essentially a failure. They do their best to study and get good grades on most of the papers they get back. Their assignment feedback usually has nothing but nice things to say. However, this student is deeply insecure. They believe they are not intelligent enough. They think that they are dumber than everybody else in their class, and despite them being at the top of their class, they feel like a phony or fake. They think they are an imposter and don't feel confident in what they do, even when they get good grades. They don't celebrate their wins because they believe perfection is the lowest standard.

Even though they get nothing but positive feedback for the most part, they still can't help but have this inherent belief that they are not good enough. When people *do* give them compliments, they don't believe them. They think other people are lying or simply being nice for the sake of being nice.

One day, they get a paper back, and their worst fear has come true. It's a B-. Their teacher gives them feedback, and some of it isn't positive. What this feedback ends up doing is validating every single negative belief they have about themselves. They think to themselves, *If this teacher believes that my paper isn't good enough, that must mean everybody else must not think I'm good enough.* All of their insecurities suddenly validate the worst things they believe about themselves.

One negative criticism does not inherently mean you are flawed! If that is the philosophy you're going to live by, then you must believe that one *positive* form of feedback means you are perfect (but we don't often think that way).

We can't let ourselves fall into the mindset that one form of criticism validates everything else we feel.

The mistakes that we've made in our past are beautiful moments in life where we learned amazing lessons that might not have been as effective had we not lived through the worst-case scenario in the first place.

Accept things as they come into your life, and any negative things that happen will become much less painful once you learn to embrace imperfections. The world is a crazy, nonsensical place. Sometimes, you try to assign sense to that, and it results in negativity and us being harsh on ourselves. There's no formula for being a perfect human. There's no handbook for how we are supposed to act. We just have to follow our innate human nature and our intuition to become the happy people that we deserve to be.

In Summary

Your future is in your hands. You might have been defined by others in the past, but now it is your decision to mold the person you want to be. Keep these things in mind:

- You have to decide to make a change and put steps in place to get the things you want; you can't wait for someone else to do that for you.

- Identify the things that you want to prioritize in your life and forget about anything that gets in the way.

- Create your own boundaries and then follow through with those by respecting them.

- Master the art of embracing your imperfections to live a more freeing life.

- Forgive yourself for the past to help you move on to a better future.

- Accept that this is the life you have, and you'll learn how to make more room for self-love.

Now you have a choice: Will you take steps to love yourself or continue repeating the same habits stemming from self-hatred?

Chapter 4:

Be Your Own Savior

Who comes to mind when you think of a heroic person? When we were kids, this image might've looked different depending on what you believe made a strong person. But now that we are older, we know the image of superheroes we've held doesn't match reality. Heroic people don't have to have special powers or be especially physically strong. Strength comes from standing up for what is right. Superheroes are those who know what the right thing to do is and are willing to do it, even if that means making sacrifices or working hard.

Now, it's time for you to be your own superhero.

Be the savior in your own story. Be ready for any occasion or obstacle. Be willing to do what needs to be done.

Trusting in yourself means letting go of fear of the future. If you believe you are capable, you believe you can make it through no matter what life throws your way. This makes you less resistant to fear and more willing to take the risks you need to take to receive amazing things.

Your Duty

You are the one you've been waiting for—you are the only one who can save yourself. Waiting around for someone else to do it will leave you longing for more and resenting yourself. Be comfortable with your situation now, and be patient with change as you take the steps to improve. You will be so grateful for yourself at the end of it all, making you your own biggest hero.

Be Uplifting

In the past, you might have depended on other people for your happiness. Perhaps you wait for others to tell you what direction to take in life, or maybe you need validation from others to know that you're a good person who deserves love no matter what. It's your duty to be your own superhero. You have to be the one who tells yourself that you are good enough and that you are accepting of who you are.

Don't be so harsh on yourself. What if the person that you looked up to the most berated you? What if they put you down and constantly made fun of you? Would you believe anything they had to say? Would you think that they were a good person? Chances are, you wouldn't. Heroes don't berate the people they save. They don't put them down and make fun of them. They aren't bullies. They uplift people around them. They make the right decisions. This is the mindset that you have to create for yourself. Inside our minds, we have many different voices. Sometimes, that voice tells us to go for it and to take a chance. Other times, that voice tells us to stop what we're doing and do something different because we aren't capable.

That voice can either uplift us or push us down and make us feel bad about ourselves. When we berate people or put them down, we destroy trust. How can you trust somebody who isn't nice to you? How can you trust somebody who makes you feel bad about yourself? This is why it can be difficult to trust ourselves and uphold that belief system that we talked about previously. You have to *believe* that you deserve to get the things that you want, and that requires trusting in yourself.

Be kind and forgiving, and uplift yourself. Train your mind to silence that inner critic. Why would you ever trust somebody who says such negative things? Why would you ever follow what they say or believe in what they have to tell you when they are surrounded by so much negativity?

You likely wouldn't think highly of a judgmental person in real life, so why do you listen so intently to the one that's in your head? If somebody walked into your home and started criticizing everything around you, you would think they had issues. You would think, *Why are they so miserable? Why aren't they able to be happy? Why are they so judgmental?*

Everybody has criticisms here and there, but somebody who is so inherently negative isn't somebody who has very solid values and perspectives that uphold and uplift us. Choose to hear the positive voice in your mind and turn down the volume on the negativity. Turn the volume up on reason and logic to prevent yourself from falling for the most limiting beliefs you have.

Sometimes, switching from a negative perspective to a more positive and uplifting one can be unrealistic for people. If you are very pessimistic and self-critical and have been that way your whole life, then when you wake up tomorrow, it's not going to be easy to switch.

To start, what can help is to be neutral. Imagine you're walking down the street, and you pass somebody, and they trip and fall. What would you do? Would you laugh at them and point and call them names? No, you likely wouldn't. When someone needs help, you'd likely ask, *Are you okay? Do you need anything?*

You have to do this for yourself. Lift yourself up. Ask what you need and ask how you need help. From there, you can start to build a foundation for being more positive and adding more love to your life. Tomorrow, when you wake up and look in the mirror, you might not feel completely happy with what's there. You've been trained to hate yourself. It's been something that's ingrained in you day after day for years, so it's going to take some time to undo all that hatred, but that's where feelings of being uplifted come into play.

Find a neutral standpoint. That is where acceptance can come in to help. When you look in the mirror tomorrow and think, *Wow, I really hate myself*, turn that into something neutral. Look in the mirror and say, *I'm feeling very unhappy about myself today, but that's okay. Things will change.*

Be honest, but stay neutral, and use self-love to help support yourself.

Think about your goals and how self-love can help you get there. You want to be happy with what you see! Accept who you are, and instead of saying in the mirror, *I hate myself*, say, *This is who I am*. Eventually, you

43

will get to a point where you are able to say, *I love myself*. Don't force that love right now if it doesn't feel authentic. Authentic love will be what heals, and it may be slightly slow to build, but it will eventually get there. Start turning down the volume on the hatred, and once it's quiet, that's when you have more space to turn up the volume on self-love.

Learn From Mistakes

Next up, it's important for us to learn from our mistakes. Not only do you have to first accept your mistakes and all of the imperfections they've brought, but now it's time to find a morsel of truth within the decisions you've made. What do these mistakes say about what you need? What do these mistakes say about what your life is lacking?

Use your mistakes to highlight a lesson you've learned because that will help carry you forward. Redesign your belief patterns to see how bad experiences are teachable moments. Know that you are more than your biggest mistakes and accept that there's no turning back. Once that's done, finding important lessons that will change your perspective for good is much easier. The sooner that you're able to do this, the easier it will become to take risks and be proactive with challenges because you will reduce the fear you have over potential failure. Rather than seeing mistakes as the scariest or worst thing you can possibly do, you'll understand that these mistakes are learning lessons. A mistake can still be a win if you learn how to use it to help you grow.

Think of it in the simplest form. You're at a restaurant with a friend. You don't know what to order on the menu. You each decide to order an entree. As they come out, you feel regretful. You wish you hadn't ordered your dish because your friend ordered something that looks delicious, and you're jealous of them. In this situation, you wouldn't beat yourself up for weeks over that choice. Instead, you think, *I wish I would have ordered something different, and next time I will*. Then, when you go to the restaurant, you know what not to order. It's a simple lesson, and we've lived through that many times before.

Now, you have to apply this simple philosophy to bigger issues. Let's say you married somebody too soon. You didn't give yourself enough time to get to know them, and now, as you're living together, you think to yourself, *Things aren't working out that great.* You become very regretful. You wish you had made different choices. You're upset with yourself, and you start to hate yourself for these decisions that you've made.

However, rather than living in regret and hoping things change, it's time to acknowledge this mistake and make amends. You can end the relationship or take steps to help improve the relationship with something like couple's counseling. You can figure out what you shouldn't have done so that in your next relationship, you can slow things down and take the necessary steps to build a relationship that lasts. Lessons can be very valuable, so find one within your mistakes to learn to appreciate what knowledge you've gained rather than getting stuck in regret over the choices you made.

Dig Deeper

Dig deep to understand yourself. You know what's on the surface, and you know what's inside. But what do those roots look like? Sometimes, we don't want to face the truth because it is painful. There might be things blocking us from seeing those roots that we have to get through first. But now you have the power to keep digging and understand further to allow you to heal in unimaginable ways.

Find alignment by understanding what drives you and what persuades your perspective. Knowing your roots means recognizing your influences and how those lead you to think, feel, and act a certain way.

Get to know your motivations, and you'll better prepare for your actions in the future, thus stopping impulsivity or self-sabotage before it happens. Know what drives you and prioritize this, and then you'll become best friends with your future self, too. When we tap into these areas of ourselves, we gain an understanding of how our brains operate, thus allowing us to maintain control over our future.

Understand Your Roots

To love ourselves, we have to understand ourselves, embrace who we are, and accept the things that we've been through. Reflection is important. Reflection means looking back on the past and connecting it to the way that it has influenced the present and will continue to influence the future. Once we raise awareness over that and become more accepting of this, it then becomes easier to make room to love ourselves. Start by tapping into what has driven negativity in your life in the past. Think back to the initial roots of when you learned to hate yourself. Unfortunately, for many of us, our family becomes our first bullies. Did you have a parent that put you down? Did you have siblings who made fun of you? Think about neighborhood kids and people at school. Sometimes, when we are children, during those very essential developmental phases, we are taught to hate ourselves. When you're taught this type of hatred at such a young age, it can become a part of you, especially when it's reinforced throughout your developmental stages. Parental figures, communities, and pop culture all influence us, so dig deep to see what other factors play a role in developing who you are as a person.

You are your own person, and while the past has influenced who you are today, it doesn't *define* who you are today. Don't shy away from the truth just because you don't like what you see.

As you start reflecting, you may realize some things about yourself, and you might start to uncover some truths that aren't necessarily things that you'd like to think about. Maybe it's difficult to admit that something impacted you more than you thought it would, or perhaps you are upset that someone from your past still has such a hold on you. However, embrace this part of yourself because it will help you become closer and recognize who you are as a person.

Confront these truths about yourself and move on. Don't ruminate too long; remember that sometimes guilt is our attempt at controlling the future. Look at the past, but maintain balance in your own life in the present. Make these connections and dig deep to the root because if you want to pull a weed out of your life, you have to get to the root. If you simply cut the head off and try to throw dirt over it to hide this weed, it will keep growing back. You have to dig from the root and pull it out that way because that can sometimes help you realize that you don't believe these things about yourself that you've been taught all your life.

For example, perhaps as you were a kid growing up, people always made fun of you for being clumsy. You weren't particularly good at sports, you always messed up, you often broke things, and it has impacted your life. People made fun of you, and they called you names. Now, as an adult, you believe these things are true. Even though you've made changes in your life and you're not the same person you used to be, you can't help but hear those past voices creep into your head, especially at times when you're feeling vulnerable or insecure. However, if you dig to the root and recognize some of the things that people have said to you in the past, you'll make some very important realizations.

For example, maybe one of your parents made fun of you, and now, as an adult and even a parent yourself, you realize that you would never say the same thing to your child that they said to you. This realization can help you understand that those insults have no validity in your life. You weren't the problem—your parent was for not uplifting you and making you feel good about yourself. Confronting the past can sometimes be difficult at first, but if you push through those emotions and reconnect with your inner child and who you used to be, it can be very freeing. It can be very comforting, and it's a way to help you nurture yourself and build emotional resilience.

Show Gratitude for Your Uniqueness

We've been taught all of our lives to be grateful. You're grateful to strangers when you say thank you if they held the door open for you. You say what you're grateful for during holidays and special occasions when you share cards with your loved ones. You show gratitude in the face of tragedy, thankful for making it out alive.

But true gratitude goes deeper than that. Research shows that gratitude can positively impact our overall health and wellness and that certain parts of our brain are activated when we experience gratitude (Allen, 2018).

Showing gratitude for who you are is the ultimate way to show self-love. Gratitude is the recognition that you are happy for every unique quality about yourself.

Admire what you see in the mirror and be appreciative of what's inside you. You are incredibly unique. There is no one in the world who is like you. Maybe you look like somebody, such as a parent or a sibling, but you are still your own person. Even identical twins can be vastly different from one another. Embrace those unique qualities because even if you might feel as though you're not conventionally attractive or you don't fit certain beauty standards, there are plenty of people in the world who think you are beautiful. You have to be grateful for what you see and be appreciative of your uniqueness because if not, you're failing to acknowledge yourself.

When you fail to acknowledge yourself, you're not going to take care of yourself. You're not going to fulfill your basic needs, and that is only going to do even more damage. This will only breed more negative thoughts, driving you further from yourself. We often wish things from our past were different, but we tend to focus on positive outcomes. You think to yourself that if only you had done something differently, then life might be better now. However, in the past, you made many decisions, and if you had made a different decision, maybe things would actually be worse than they are now.

We like to think that if only we had done a certain thing differently, everything would be fine. However, if only we *hadn't* done a certain thing in the past, maybe our lives would have been ruined!

If you're going to live in a positive world that doesn't exist, where all of your decisions would have led to a better life, you have to stay grounded in reality and recognize that things could have easily been much worse than they are now.

Sure, a simple decision could've changed your life for the better, but it also could have changed your life for the worse. For example, consider someone who went to trade school for a two-year degree. They think to themselves, *I should've worked harder and become a doctor. I should have studied more and partied less.*

However, if this person had decided to pursue a doctorate degree, something worse could have happened on this path. They could've had a mental breakdown from all the stress of studying and dropped out of school, not getting a degree at all. Perhaps they did become a doctor but realized they hated that job and weren't good at it. They don't give patients the care they need and end up hurting people in the process.

Things could be worse, so when you get stuck in a "Grass-is-greener" mentality, where you're always fantasizing about how things could have been better, stay grounded in reality and remind yourself that things could have been worse. The pendulum swings both ways, so we have to have the power to be grateful and appreciative for what we have and who we are now.

In Summary

You are your biggest hero, so start acting accordingly. To do that, follow these steps:

- Know that it's your duty to take the front seat of your life and move to the things you want rather than sitting back and hoping they'll fall into your lap.

- Be uplifting to yourself; superheroes aren't rude and degrading.

- Learn from your biggest mistakes and find a lesson in each regret you have.

- Dive into your past to start making connections to the things that taught you that you were undeserving of love.

- Know that there is no one else like you, and practice gratitude for your unique self.

Unleash your inner hero and let the superhero within you carry you to the place you want to be.

Chapter 5:

Unleash the Real You Under

All the Bravado

You're driven by two things:

- primal human instincts

- moral, ethical, and societal standards

The combination of these two creates your ego (Cherry, 2023). All day long, we're presented with choices that we have to navigate and decisions that could alter our direction in life. Our ego has to balance what comes as a natural urge and what we've been taught.

Think of it like this: It's a hot summer day, and your sweet tooth leads you to the local ice cream shop. You walk in, and your hunger awakens, making you want to order a large banana split with extra toppings—this is your primal urge. You then think to yourself about how you don't need all that much, so maybe you should just get an extra small vanilla—these are the standards you've been taught.

Your ego aims to strike a balance, assessing your hunger levels and anything else you ate that day to help you make a decision as to what you want.

In everyday life, our ego is in a constant battle between our natural urges and our second-guessing. If you struggle to love yourself, chances are, you're finding it difficult to cool the deep-rooted urges in you and can't seem to get everyone else's thoughts and words out of your head. You might feel pulled in many directions, unsure of which way to head next. When the ego runs wild, it drags us around with it, leaving us feeling defeated and out of control.

Tame your ego. Find your true self and dismiss the bravado. Discover your innate human nature to connect back to what matters most.

Your Challenge

Letting go of our ego is one of the biggest challenges we might face. Our ego is built over time, like a brick wall that society and communities place down, which may make us feel trapped inside. Pressure from society to look a certain way, influence from families, and shame instilled from social circles may create our identities. Sometimes, we might not like the person we've been shaped into, so we must learn to shed the ego and set free the person we are meant to be.

The Ego Blocks Love

We don't get a lot of love from society. We get love from our friends and family, but the people around us don't give us the kind of love we need to fulfill our needs and make us feel whole. Instead, what we get from society are judgments, preconceived notions, impossible standards, and other rules that are very hard for people to follow. Society creates this image of what a perfect individual should look like, and if we even step slightly outside that box, it can make our experiences and lives much more difficult.

The ego is built over time, and it is separated from love because our ego, fear, doubt, and self-centeredness can prevent true love from happening, whether it's directed at ourselves or others. For example, we might fear who we are. We fear we are not good enough. We fear we are not lovable. We fear we are imposters and not being true to who we are. We constantly doubt ourselves. We doubt if what we believe is true. We doubt if we are intelligent enough or good enough to do our jobs. We doubt if we are capable of getting good things in our life. Self-centeredness makes us feel like the world is out to get us. We think other people are judging us and that they're thinking about us way more than they are. We think other people are hurting us when they neglect our needs, and we take things as insults, even when the other person never meant to hurt us in any way.

When we center ourselves in the world, it makes us feel very disconnected because the world is not created for the individual. The world is created by centuries of societies crafting rules and ideologies that influence us from the moment we're born.

Love requires vulnerability. It requires honesty, truth, and authenticity, and those are all things that society teaches us to block throughout our lives. Love requires sacrifice and making difficult decisions that might not benefit us in the end. Love requires acknowledgment, appreciation, and acceptance of who we are and our deepest flaws. There are so many challenging things that we might not be ready for because the world hasn't prepared us to love ourselves. The world is brutal; it is intense; it is competitive, and all of these things can make it difficult for us to live our truest, most authentic lives. Your ego has created this brick wall that has blocked love from thriving because not only is that what you've been taught, but it's what you needed to do to survive.

You are a garden. To let a garden grow and thrive, it needs space. Plants need to be able to stretch their roots. Some plants need support, like trellises or stakes, to help them thrive. Plants need attention, and they need nourishment. Society puts us in a box, and we can't grow in that box. Throughout our lives, we spend time keeping that box closed because it's what we think we're supposed to do. Let yourself grow. Open that box, let your garden thrive, let your guard down, and release these blockages because that will open you up to more fulfilling relationships, whether that relationship is with yourself or with other people. Stop blocking love from your life.

It's instinctual to block love. We have these instincts wired in us all of our lives. When you see somebody about to drop something or fall, you reach your arms out to catch them. When the sun is glaring in your eyes, you stick your hand up to block the sun. When you're hungry, you reach for food. When you're thirsty, you reach for water. These are all instincts, and one instinct we don't realize we have is the instinct to block love. It's hard to be vulnerable when you put yourself out there. It can be scary to share your emotions and live your truest self. When you are authentic, some people aren't going to like that. They will make fun of you. They will put you down. They will make you feel crazy for being authentic. They will make you feel like you're the weird one for being the truest form of yourself. Let go of that instinct to block who you are, deep down, so that you can let love live and flourish.

Shed Your Ego

Shed your ego and look for the new you. There's a version of you that society has created. This version is scared, angry, and resentful because they have been blocked all their life, and that creates a whole new type of person. Let your authentic self flourish. This means forgiving yourself for stifling who you truly are. This means forgiving yourself for being so hard on yourself and putting yourself in that box.

We have to forgive ourselves for prioritizing our needs last and putting other people first. We have to forgive ourselves for highlighting bad memories and forgetting positive memories. Now, there is a new version of you, and this person is ready to embrace and accept love in their life. Stay focused on yourself, but remember not to do this at the expense of others. Yes, you need to prioritize yourself, but we also still live in a society where everyone is like you. They deserve love, they deserve support, and they deserve to have their needs met. Be a light in your life and a light that shines in others, not somebody who dims the light of others.

You can exist as who you want to be. Anyone who has a problem with this has to deal with that problem on their own. Anyone who doesn't like you and doesn't agree with what you believe or what you stand for has their own issues to work out. You can't make other people happy. Even if you become a version of yourself that somebody else wants you to be, that still isn't enough to make them happy because we all have this inherent responsibility to make ourselves happy. We all have the responsibility to make choices that prioritize our own needs, so when you focus on prioritizing somebody else, not only are you hurting yourself, but you're not doing them any favors either. Being someone you're not is not going to help them. You can't heal somebody else.

You can't change the way somebody else thinks. You can only influence people and be a positive light and hope that maybe they'll follow you on your path to healing. You can't stifle who you are just to satisfy someone else.

Be you! Redefine your ego and let that light flourish. Stop dimming your growth and stop stifling positive change. Make a choice each and every day to water your garden and let yourself bloom.

Humanity and Nature

Love elevates us. Giving into your humanity will make it easier to embrace nature and all its ups and downs. No one truly knows what it means to be a perfect human; we are all doing the best we can and figuring things out as we go. Embrace this concept in your day-to-day life to make it easier to overcome doubt, self-deprecation, and disappointment with yourself.

Association

Support isn't essential on the road to self-love. You can do this on your own. However, it's important to remember that you grow with the people you surround yourself with.

While you can't control other people, and other people can't control you, there are influences that persuade our way of thinking and acting, so it's crucial to choose people who are positive and who uplift you rather than people who might be negative and bring you down.

If somebody's negative or unhappy, you don't have to cut them out of your life. If that were the case, then many of us wouldn't have any friends. However, you don't have to let their negativity influence you. They might have very damaging world views, but you don't have to believe those things as well. You can do this without others, and you can do this with others. You can learn to work and grow with people in the process, or you can learn to work and grow on your own. There are no rules for self-growth.

However, you have to remember what it means to be self-sufficient versus what it means to be dependent on other people. The words that other people say can creep into your psyche, and if you're not aware, then they can unconsciously influence you. Know the difference between unconditional and conditional love, and the rest will sort itself out.

Choose people in your life who are good and who make you happy. Choose people who uplift you, and even if they might be going through their own things and aren't able to help you, ensure that they aren't actively trying to bring you down.

Remember that other people have intentions that we can't comprehend. We don't know what's going on in their mind. We don't know what's motivating them or influencing them. While somebody might seem like they're being negative or they are trying to break you down, that's not always the case. Other people aren't out to get you. They might be resentful, or they might be jealous, but at the end of the day, we are all humans. We all have that inherent humanity within us that makes us want to protect ourselves and ensure that our needs are met. How people go about that can be strange and confusing. We might not understand what influences somebody. We might not understand why they don't change, especially if we can see how they could improve their own lives. But ultimately, it's not for us to decide how somebody else lives their life, so we have to remember to keep focusing on ourselves.

If you find that you are struggling with negativity or you feel really insecure, look at the people around you in your life. Look at their influence. Is somebody negative to you? Do they call you names? Do they make passive-aggressive remarks? Do they make snarky comments? Again, you don't have to cut everybody else who's negative. Sometimes people might say things that come out harsher than they intended, and other people do make mistakes. They say things they shouldn't. That doesn't mean that we have to end a relationship, but look at consistency. How frequently are they doing this? If you are afraid to hang out with somebody because you know that every time they make a sassy comment, maybe it's good to limit the relationship that you have with them. If somebody says something mean to you one time, you don't have to cut them out of your life. However, address these concerns with other people and see how they react. If somebody is willing to improve, apologize, and take accountability, then you can still have a good relationship with them. Sometimes, relationships with conflict end up being the strongest when two people can communicate and effectively put attention into their relationship to grow.

The Natural Flow

Remember that with nature comes a natural flow of life. We can't rush time, and we can't alter time. Time is the one thing that will always be out of our control. Learn to have patience and trust in the natural flow of the universe.

This relates to humanity in that you need to be patient because other people aren't going to change at the same rate as you. You might have to be patient because people are still struggling and they're still growing. They're still in the phase where they hate themselves, and they will take that out on you. However, notice small changes because some people just might not grow as fast as you.

When you're vulnerable, you're given unmatched strength. When you open yourself up and you tell somebody, *Hey, you hurt me*, it can be scary. What if they laugh at you? What if they dismiss your feelings? What if they make you feel worse than you already do? However, that is a sign of strength that we don't always recognize because of our ego and because of the world that we live in. But when you're vulnerable like that, you're showing somebody that you're not going to stand for what they have to say. You're addressing this conflict, and you're not going to let these repeated patterns keep happening. When you permit yourself to be human, you can connect back to the world around you.

You recognize the intricacies within nature and how they influence the uniqueness of the world. Embracing this ideology allows you more room to love yourself and less emphasis on regret. You can't change people's perceptions of you. How they view you is always going to be dependent on their own issues and the things that they've been through. That's part of human nature. If you learn to embrace and accept this, it alleviates your life. It makes things so much easier. It's not that you shouldn't care what other people think all the time, because sometimes their opinions *do* matter. If you respect somebody and you understand that somebody is intelligent, of course, you're going to want them to understand you and respect you back. However, when somebody thinks so negatively about you, or you worry that they're harshly judging you, you have to remember that, at the end of the day, maybe they are—and that's okay because that's their perspective, and that's the life that they've lived.

What others think of you doesn't have to change what you think of yourself.

You have the ability to love yourself already within you. Unleash this ability and let go of what society has stifled within you or what society has made you feel is wrong. Let yourself flourish and be the truest form of who you are that you can possibly be.

In Summary

Forget what others have taught you to believe about yourself; you know who you are and what things you want to gain in this life. Let go of your ego by remembering:

- Knock down the brick wall that society has forced you to build and enjoy the fresh air on your face as you step outside of this rigid box!

- Question the things that make you want to uphold this ego to help you let go and shed that ego once and for all.

- Remember that you're a unique part of human nature, so tap into your roots and connect to your deepest human qualities.

- The people around you will influence who you become; we learn certain traits by association, so be cognizant of their influence.

- Remember, there is a natural flow to the universe and balance in the world, so trust that time will carry you to where you are supposed to be.

For so long, the real you has been tucked away, deep inside, and waiting for this moment to finally be free.

Chapter 6:

Reignite the Relationship You

Have With Yourself

Humans are born to be social creatures, but ultimately, we are often alone. We are alone with our thoughts when feeling anxious and nervous. We are alone when we go to sleep at night, even if we do share a bed with someone, only we can understand our thoughts and feelings.

Our experiences, while shared, are unique to us and our perspective. For this reason, it's essential that we learn how to love ourselves. Ask yourself:

- When was the last time you saw a movie or play at the theater by yourself?

- When was the last time you took yourself out to dinner alone at a restaurant?

- How often do you enjoy spending nights alone?

You might be alone often, but do you actually enjoy these moments? Learn how to have a relationship with yourself.

Surround yourself with love and become fearless. Life will never let up, so accept yourself now and set firm boundaries. Embrace, accept, and make friends with the person you were from your past—mistakes and all.

Your Relationship

Accept yourself on the inside. You will always be on your own side. You will always have yourself, no matter who comes in and out of your life. You can never know someone else as intimately as you know yourself. You have to learn how to like yourself and repair the relationship you have so you can live life happier and more freely.

Own Up

We've talked about why it's important to take accountability and own up, but now, how can you actually do that? At the end of the day, most of us know that deep down, it's important to admit that we're wrong and own up, but what does that admission actually look like? How can we admit we're wrong without having to take the blame for everything, especially in situations where others were also wrong? How do we admit we made mistakes in situations where we weren't taught differently or might not have known better? These situations can block us from taking necessary steps to accountability because there's a feeling that if we admit one thing is wrong, then all things are wrong.

In our world, competition can make us sometimes feel like there's a winner and a loser. That's true when we're talking about sports; one team wins, the other team loses. But even in sports, there can still be ties!

You can have an argument with somebody or a conversation where one person is right while the other person is *also* right. There's not always a balance where one person has to be wrong, and the other person has to be right. Conversations aren't about winning the conversation and proving your point better than the other person. Conversations should be about two people sharing ideas and listening to each other.

To help you start owning up more, remember to be real. Own up to the mistakes you've made in the past. However, learn how to strike a balance between owning up and also still loving yourself. Don't let the imperfect spoil the perfect. The pressure to want to be the best or know it all is intense, and that can turn us away from the truth. If we admit that we're wrong about one thing, does that mean that we have to admit that we're wrong about *everything*? If we admit that we're wrong, does that mean we don't know what we're talking about? We may tend to become afraid to admit that we're wrong because we don't want people to think less of us. We don't want to come off as somebody who's untrustworthy. We fear our authority gets lost if we own up or admit that we did something wrong. However, that's not the case! The ability to shed the ego and own up can actually be a sign of strength!

To help you learn how to own up, start by addressing the main overarching problems in your life. Stop dodging these problems. This means that in the past, if you've wondered if you're making bad choices, look directly at those choices now and know that it's time to change.

Sometimes, we oversimplify our problems because we don't understand why they're so difficult to manage. We often confuse ourselves by making excuses or finding reasons why we can't make a change. We tell ourselves:

- *Oh, I'll wait until the beginning of the month to start a new workout routine.*

- *It'll be easier to start off fresh on a brand-new month.*

- *I'll wait until after the holidays to start working on my manuscript.*

- *Once I get this problem fixed, then I'll be able to focus on this other problem.*

This kind of mentality is a form of procrastination. At the end of the day, there is always going to be an excuse why we can't do something or why waiting until later is better. You don't have to wait until Monday to start a new life. You don't have to wait until you meet certain expectations to start living your life and be happy. Stop dodging these problems and recognize them now. Admit why you might be pushing them off and why procrastination might be the norm for you.

The tricky part is balancing this acknowledgment without slipping into a pit of self-blame.

If you start saying things like:

- Maybe I need to work a little bit harder.

- Maybe I need to take better care of myself.

- Maybe I should've made a better decision.

Then, you might start to turn against yourself, putting yourself down for the choices you made.

You might say:

- Why didn't I do this sooner?

- Why did I make things so much harder for myself?

- Why did I push things off until the last minute?

That's when you have to take steps to practically stop your mind from going down that path to where you turn toward self-blame.

Let go of the past, remember to practice self-forgiveness, and remember that you didn't know then what you know now. Now you know, so now you can make changes. You didn't have the same perspective that you have now, but now that you do know, it's time to take responsibility. Don't blame your past self. Instead, have compassion for them.

Understand them, love them, and show them that you care now. Take that same philosophy and apply it to your future self. Show you love them and show you care by making good decisions and making choices to help set you up for the future. There's a balance between knowing that you need to be hard on yourself and using some tough love to actually make a change versus blaming yourself and getting stuck in agony over wishing you had made changes sooner.

Admit your faults and recognize that you *do* have the power to work on these. It *is* within your control to make changes. Those changes might not look perfect. They might not be exactly what you want, but change never looks how we want it to look. Consider the last time you got a haircut. Most of the time, our haircut turns out different than what we had pictured in our head. When was the last time you researched a restaurant or a hotel on the internet and saw pictures, but then, once you saw it in person, it looked so much different? The things in our heads don't always look the same as they do around us. All we can do is take small steps and make small changes, and eventually, we'll fulfill that picture that we have in our heads of what we'd like to gain.

You are who you are, and you can learn to like that about yourself.

You don't have to change to be who you want to be. Instead, you can change to like who you already are.

Own up to what you've done, admit that it's a part of you, and use that knowledge and power for good. Be kind to your past self, forgive yourself for any mistakes you've made, and make promises to your future self that you will do what you need to do to live the life you want.

Drop Opinions

Our opinions are another huge part of our lives that can hold us back and keep us from getting the things that we love. Opinions destroy the relationship that we have with ourselves. When was the last time you dated somebody new and introduced them to your friends or family? You were likely nervous about this, right? You wanted to make sure that your family liked this person. You got scared that maybe they would judge something about them. What if they judge them, and then you focus on this flaw, and now that bothers you and ruins the relationship that you have with your new partner? Other people's opinions can impact how we feel about somebody else, and that's true for how we feel about ourselves. On one hand, other people's opinions validate some of the biggest fears that we have about ourselves. For example, if you are going out and you get all dressed up, you might be having a bad hair day. Maybe you're unhappy with your outfit, and your

65

clothes fit a little differently than how they used to fit. You simply don't feel confident enough. Then, when you get there, somebody says, "Oh, your hair looks different today."

It's not necessarily a compliment, and it's not necessarily something mean, so it makes you start questioning what they mean. Are they saying it looks different because it looks bad? Are they saying it looks different because it's a weird hairstyle that you chose? You start second-guessing yourself, and you start doubting yourself, and that all of a sudden makes the rest of you feel weird. Well, if they think your hair looks weird, do they think your outfit looks weird as well? This can make us feel very anxious and self-conscious. We start picking apart the rest of our body and our appearance, wondering what other flaws other people are perceiving.

It's essential to ensure that you don't let one opinion of you ruin your upward progress, whether that comes from other people or if that comes from yourself.

Don't give power to people who don't deserve it. It's okay to take criticism from others. Sometimes, people will genuinely have some good feedback that could help you improve.

However, there should be a balance. Somebody who has nothing but negative things to say isn't trying to help you. A person who often uplifts you and gives you good advice might be more valid when they're giving feedback. Look at the balance between how somebody treats you overall and then use that to help assess the opinions they're sharing. If you notice the way that you let other people's voices creep into your head, remind yourself that you don't have to give weight to these fictionalized versions. Sometimes, we might anticipate certain things that people might say, and that can make us feel insecure and fearful. Unless somebody actually says something to you, don't take their judgment to heart. Don't let the voices or the negativity from the people around you creep into your head.

When it comes to dropping opinions, it's also crucial to avoid the comparison monster. Comparison is a trap. There's always going to be something else you can compare yourself to, and you never know anybody else's story. What you see on the outside is only what someone else wants you to see. You don't see what's going on behind the scenes where they might be struggling or hurting in ways worse than you could even imagine. Focus on yourself, what you like, and who you are, and let people deal with their own opinions. Everyone has opinions, so don't give them as much weight as you might be giving them now.

Live With Freedom

Don't live your life on expectations. Everyone else has an image of you; they don't know you as deeply as you know yourself. They place expectations on you, whether that's your parent, partner, or random stranger walking down the street. Society demands we act a certain way, and that provides us with all sorts of restrictive feelings. Live freely by ignoring these expectations and living as authentically as you can.

Your Needs First

As you start loving yourself more and begin repairing the relationship that you have with yourself, it's essential to put your needs in front of others. Give up on people pleasing. People pleasing is a form of validation that occurs when we are looking for love outside of ourselves. It's okay to be a kind person. It's good to be polite and have manners. It's also admirable to be generous and caring and make sacrifices to help other people. However, you can't do that at the expense of yourself. You also can't try to be the person who's constantly people-pleasing and trying to win the affection of somebody who doesn't care to give you that validation back.

The best way to prioritize your own needs is to set clear and definitive boundaries. Know your worth and what you want to share with the world. Anyone who is willing to neglect, ignore, or cross your boundaries isn't worth letting you into your life anymore.

To set a boundary, you first have to recognize the need that you have, and what needs to be prioritized. This might mean spending more time with your family and saying no to the constant demands of work. It could mean having alone time with your partner and nights where you two do your own things rather than spending every moment together. It could mean telling your group of friends that you no longer want to participate in gossip. Maybe you can't always be there for somebody as much as they need you. Whatever this boundary looks like, first identify the need that is getting neglected so that way you acknowledge yourself. After that, then you can start setting stronger boundaries.

What do you need to make sure that this boundary is protected? That will mean talking to other people and setting goals with them. Once you have established the need that has been neglected and then the boundary that you need to set, it's then time to share this boundary with other people. Let everybody know what you need from them and what you will no longer tolerate. Boundaries are something that we also have to set for ourselves. That means if you notice yourself ruminating or second-guessing, you cut yourself off and you focus on something else. That means if you are stuck in self-hate and you can't stop self-deprecating, you turn down the volume and tell yourself that this voice is not valid and that the negative things they are saying are not true. Boundaries are for protecting your peace and making it easier for you to ultimately love yourself in the way that you deserve.

Find Your Groove

Find your groove with the right people and choose to prioritize relationships that are good for the soul. When you surround yourself with people who are happy and who enjoy life, you will find that your own life improves in the process. Those you let go in your life also have the option to change and catch up to your mindset, improving their life in the process. We all make our own decisions, so you have to find your own groove and then go with that flow. If somebody else wants to follow and they want to change and be a better person as well, then you can invite them along on the ride. Having a supportive network can be very helpful. If they want to hold you back and prevent you from going on that groove, you need to separate yourself from them for the time being. Sometimes, distance can be helpful! If you start living a better life, you become happier, and you make changes to work on yourself, this other person might see that and become

68

inspired. They then decide that they want to make those changes themselves. That's okay, and that's actually a good thing! It means that the two of you can work together to support each other and learn from each other in the process. However, if you discover that somebody is manipulative or puts you down, then it's going to add resistance as you try to move and go with the flow.

Spread your wings and let yourself find freedom and growth. Do what makes you happy. When you start becoming fearful about losing people in your life, stop and ask yourself: *Why am I afraid of losing someone who is not going to support me on my journey?*?

What is it that you're gaining from somebody else who puts you down? What are you gaining from seeking validation from them and getting their approval? Why is it important for you to have the approval of somebody negative and unhappy with their own life?

All we can do for this type of person is hope that they come to the same conclusions you are and make positive changes for themselves. You have to let go of the opinions of other people because even if that means you end up here alone, that will be okay! It's okay to be alone. It's not a bad thing to not have a huge network of people in your life. While it is good to have socialization and some people who support you, it's not worth being surrounded by people who are negative and who put you down. It's better to have one strong friendship rather than ten friendships with people who are unhappy and don't want to see you succeed.

When you don't love yourself, then the latter sounds better. It sounds better to have multiple people who are there to validate you and approve of you, but they might not even be providing that approval. You're simply on the chase for their affection, their attention, and their approval. That chase can be exhilarating. When we get small signs that people are validating or approving of us, it can make us feel better about ourselves. But that's not a solid foundation for you to love yourself and support yourself in the way that you deserve.

When you learn to repair the relationship you have with yourself and you practice self-love in the best way possible, then what ultimately happens is it becomes easier to let go of some of those relationships that don't do anything but hold you back. You'll realize that you don't care what other people think. You'll start to question why it mattered to you so much in the past. When you focus on yourself, your own needs, and your own goals, then you can actually start achieving those goals. When you instead are focused on getting the approval of others, proving people wrong, and seeking validation, then you're never going to reach your goals, and you're not going to get that validation you're so desperately wanting, either.

Instead, you'll be left feeling lonely and hating yourself. Focus on yourself and put your own needs first. Again, if people want to join you on your journey, then at the end of the day, when you reach your goals, not only will you be happy with your success, but you'll also have people in your life who matter the most.

In Summary

There's no one in this world that you'll spend more time with than yourself! Learn to love this person, or life will be much harder for you. To help reignite the relationship you have with yourself, remember these key elements:

- Own up to the things you did in the past that you might not be completely proud of, as this will release some of the resentment you have for yourself.

- Forget the opinions that others have placed on you and identify how these have impacted your ability to love yourself.

- Live life based on your own expectations and shed the limitations that others have put in place for you.

- Identify your needs and then let these become your main focal point in the days ahead.

- Go with the flow and find your groove; don't follow anyone else's.

There's no relationship more unique than the one you have with yourself. Learn how to cherish this, as that is the first step in creating a strong foundation for self-love.

Chapter 7:

Illuminate Your Path to Happiness

Countless studies have tried to determine what it means to be happy. What is found is often surprising for researchers. There's no clear indication of happiness or marker we can use to undoubtedly determine if someone is happy or unhappy. It doesn't matter what someone's characteristics, economic standing, or cultural background are; the only thing that can wholly determine happiness is the individual.

This serves as a reminder that there's nothing we need to get, buy, or achieve to be happy. The ability already exists within us; we just have to learn how to unleash that happiness. While it is within our control to feel a certain way, it's no easy feat. But with the right steps, you will learn how to decode the happiness waiting to be embraced.

Discover the secret to true happiness. Let go of control and embrace the chaos of the world because only then will you be able to fully rejoice in the beauty that surrounds you.

Your Happiness

Unlock the love that's already within you. You're human, meaning you're built with the power of love. Don't let all of that potential go to waste. Think back to a time when you felt an overwhelming, overpowering, destructive, negative emotion. As much power as that emotion had is how much power you are capable of giving to love.

It's Already in You

Up until this point, the problem with self-love has likely been that you've been looking around you and outside of you to try to find love, but in reality, self-love already exists *inside* you. You have the ability to illuminate your path to happiness. Only *you* can decide what you want. Only *you* can decide what will actually fulfill you. You can pretend you're happy on the outside. You can tell people that you're happy. But deep down, only *you* will ever be able to actually feel that happiness and know what it takes to maintain those emotions. Be ready to receive love from yourself and the people around you.

To embrace love, first, you have to accept the idea that you are deserving of love and that you are already capable of doing it. You might think to yourself, *I don't have any self-love. That's why I'm here!*

Well, in reality, the fact that you're here is exact proof that you do have the capabilities to love yourself. What is it that makes you feel like you're undeserving of love? Whatever thoughts pop into your head are invalid because you deserve love. That's the simple truth.

There's nothing in this world that exists that would be valid proof that you don't deserve love. Is it somebody else's opinion? Is it something that you've formulated yourself over time? Is it an experience you had or something you did that you regret that makes you think that you're not deserving of love? We all deserve love, and we all have the power to give love to ourselves, so whenever those thoughts pop in that tell you that you don't deserve love, know that it is wrong.

Start by identifying some of the acts of self-love that you already have shown yourself. Look around your house. Do you keep the space organized? Do you have decorations? Do you fill it with things that you love? These are all forms of proof that you care about yourself. You've been loving yourself unknowingly all this time; now is the opportunity to take those pieces of evidence that you love yourself and amplify them. How can you make your space even more inviting? How can you take even better care of yourself?

Look at some of those things you've done, and then ask yourself if you did that because you *want* to or because you feel like you should. Did somebody tell you that you need to work out and eat healthy, so that's why you do now? If so, change your motives and remind yourself that you're doing these things not just because somebody told you to do them but because you deserve them and because you know that that's what you need to live a happy and wholesome life.

Love Is Contagious

We already know that hatred and negativity are contagious. When you're having a good day, your vibes are strong, and positivity is flowing, then one bad thing can really ruin the rest of your day. Whether that means getting stuck in traffic, stubbing your toe, spilling coffee on your shirt, or being around somebody in a bad mood, it doesn't take a lot to damper positivity. We know this to be true, but now we have to take that truth and flip it oppositely. Love is just as contagious as hate. Positivity is just as easily spread as negativity is. Your love shines a light on other people.

It can be hard to be positive because we might be surrounded by so many negative people. We tend to be around people who are similar to us and who might be in the same kind of situation. For example, if you grew up in poverty, then chances are you have some friends who also grew up in poverty. You might be an outlier in your group, but for the most part, we can sometimes be in the same circle as individuals who are struggling like us.

Aside from parts of our lives like economic standing, personal interests, and hobbies, we are often close to those who have personalities similar to ours. You may find that if you're a negative, unhappy person who struggles with self-love, then the people who are around you are also doing the same. It can be hard to change because we don't want to be the outlier in a group. We don't want to be the person who invalidates somebody else's experiences. We might not want to change that much either because we've been in the same kind of circle for so long that it can feel strange or awkward to change when everybody else is doing the same thing. However, your love can shine a light. It can become contagious! As you start to improve self-love and repair your relationship with yourself, two things could happen. On one hand, people see that light, and they try to dim it. They get jealous.

They don't understand how to love themselves, and they see you loving yourself, and they want that to stop. If you love yourself, then that means it's actually possible to love yourself and live a happy life, which can invalidate everything you believe. They might be stuck in a self-blaming cycle and put responsibility on everybody around them and not take accountability for their actions. When you start taking accountability for your actions and making positive changes, that can make the other person feel panicked. They don't want to have to do the same thing that you're doing. They aren't willing to make sacrifices and put the work in.

But, the other thing that might happen is that people are *inspired* by you. They see you changing, and they think, "Wow, I could change too."

Your bond then becomes stronger, and both of you grow and improve. As this starts to happen, it's crucial to know the difference between somebody who wants to step into your light and turn on theirs as well versus somebody who's trying to dim your light.

Once you know the difference, it becomes easier to protect your peace and also help people out in the process. Positivity spreads, so immerse yourself in this positive atmosphere.

A smile can make a day, even if that means making your own day. Look in the mirror when you wake up in the morning and just smile at yourself once; it might feel crazy, but so is living the whole day negativity. Smile at yourself because this can make you feel better. Smile at other people, and you'll realize that people start smiling back. Not everybody will, and that's okay. They don't have to. However, as you start to spread that positivity, it can inspire you to keep going, giving you more motivation to keep pushing through the negative and building the positive.

Time to Love Yourself

Take steps to love yourself. Do something every day to be proud of! Get what you want, and forget the rest.

Make small goals and set them, celebrating each and every one. Make time to dedicate to just yourself and no one else. Do things you love to do and rejoice in these moments of happiness.

Remind yourself that it's okay to relax—you don't always have to be on the go. Slow down and appreciate the world around you because this will make the hard moments easier to handle. Let's look at two stages of kickstarting self-love:

- Choosing to be positive.

- Rejoicing in that positivity.

Pick Optimism

Optimism is a choice. When you meet somebody who's exuding positivity and optimism, it might seem like they have a natural quality to them. You might feel jealous, wondering what it is about them that gives them the characteristics to be capable of being so positive in such a negative world. In reality, positivity is a choice you have to make each and every day—but that's not to say it's not still a difficult decision.

Sometimes, people wince at the statement that positivity is a choice. Saying it's a choice can make it seem like negativity is a choice—and nobody chooses to be anxious, depressed, or struggling with their thoughts. Just because optimism can be a choice, that doesn't mean that negativity is a choice. This belief of positivity being a choice is not something that has to invalidate your struggles or make you feel like it's your fault that you've been depressed in the past.

Choosing to be optimistic is a decision that we can make, even when it's difficult. It's like choosing to climb a mountain or choosing to go to medical school. These things are no easy feat. They require some dedication and effort on our part. Picking optimism is difficult, but if we implement small habits throughout our day to make positivity easier, then we'll find that it starts to naturally pop up in life. Start by telling yourself more positive affirmations. What does that mean? We often say very negative things to ourselves, such as:

- *I'm not good enough.*

- *No one likes me.*

- *I'm always letting others down.*

These are all negative affirmations. They are statements that aren't necessarily true or false, but they can make us believe they are true when we repeat them over and over. They're very strong, sweeping statements that can influence the way that we think.

Start raising awareness over some of the negative affirmations you've been saying to yourself. Do you have a specific thing you focus on, such as your talents, skills, or appearance?

Once you realize just how often you repeat negative affirmations, begin twisting them and turn them into positive affirmations. For example, if you tell yourself, *I can't do this,* turn it into, *I am capable.* Change "never" into "sometimes." Turn "worst" into "best." Twist those negative affirmations to turn them into something more truthful, and you'll start to discover that you are capable of forming these positive connections in your own mind. It's the little things that matter; these small decisions that we make every day are the things that are going to make it easier to love ourselves, which means smiling at yourself in the mirror or telling a stranger to have a wonderful day. That means buying somebody flowers, even if it's not a special occasion, or calling a loved one up just to chat. It means making a better choice for your future or your family's future. It means giving and sacrificing to help add a smile to somebody else's face. Be the ever-optimist and rejoice in your wins. Be grateful for your life and the world around you, and see optimism as a strength.

Sometimes, people confuse positivity with ignorance. How could you be positive in such a negative world? That's not the case. Negativity is ignorance because it's the denial that positivity is possible. Positivity is such a strength because even in a world where such horrific things happen, you still can wake up and tell yourself each day, *I have the power to make a change.*

As you start making these small tweaks in your life and adding additional changes to your way of thinking, it can be a cognitive form of restructuring. This eventually will change the way that you can react and respond to your surroundings. Again, it's not easy at first. There are still going to be plenty of times when you wake up and just tell yourself, *I can't do it today,* but tell yourself *I will do it despite how hard it is.* Each time you say that to yourself, it will get easier and easier to make changes. One morning, you will wake up and tell yourself, *I can do this* without even having to think about it. Implement those small changes and pick optimism each day because that is the way that you will see the most change.

Rejoice and Rejuvenate

Rejoice and rejuvenate in the world around you. Find the beauty in the mundane. It can be hard to be happy and build self-love because we have such high expectations for the world around us. What we forget is that the world is filled with people who are like us and just doing their best to make decisions based on what they've been through. Life doesn't have to be magical. Movies and society can make it seem that way, but that's not the case. Social media and modern society trick us into thinking that happiness and love are different than what they really are.

You *can* find beauty and amazing things in something like a simple leaf falling from a tree. Watch a bird fly around and see what they do. Study an insect as they crawl across the ground. Appreciate the rain, even when you want sun. Let the sun shine on you, even when you feel hot. Be grateful that you can take a warm shower. Be grateful if you have a pillow and blanket to sleep with at night. Show appreciation for amazing things, no matter what they are! Even a morning cup of coffee that you have had every single day of your life can be an amazing discovery if you sit there with it in front of you and learn how to be grateful. Think about where this coffee came from and all that went into making the coffee. Think about the generations of people before you who have enjoyed coffee just like you did. Think of the way that coffee has changed the world.

When you start creating this type of rejoicing, amazing perspective, life becomes so much more interesting. You can find beauty in everything. You'll find lessons in pain, and you'll find hope in despair.

Connect to the earth. Connect to your roots and connect to your passions. Do something new and something kind for yourself. Manifest luck, and wait for it to come because it will when you make decisions to be optimistic and create a positive outlook.

In Summary

The path to happiness is already there, waiting for you to take the steps needed to follow this path. Let self-love be the light that shines down the path, leading you to exactly where you want to be.

- Know that the ability to love yourself already lies in waiting, and now it's time for you to tap into this endless pool, using it as a source for stronger self-love.

- When you practice self-love, this type of light is contagious for others, and they will be able to share and relish that love when you start spreading positivity.

- There's no time to wait to love yourself; now is your chance to take advantage of self-love and use it on your path to happiness.

- Optimism might be a difficult choice, but it's a choice you can make nonetheless, so choose this as a form of self-love.

- Practice the art of celebration and learn what it means to rejoice in happiness and build toward a rejuvenated future.

What is blocking you on your path to happiness? Tap deep into yourself to uncover these secrets so you can cultivate a happy life.

Chapter 8:

Empower Yourself with Hope

Each day, the heart beats over 100,000 times (Wells, 2017). Every beat is a reminder of how much your heart works to keep you alive. The heart does more than that, too—sometimes it might signal you to something more important. If your heart starts rapidly beating, you might get the feeling that you're nervous. If you feel relaxed and at peace, then you know you're safe.

The heart is a vital part of your body, and while it might not produce the same functions that your brain does, it can still be a cue that helps you learn more about yourself.

On the path of self-love, your heart is your compass. Find your true self in the moment. Find the strength in choosing to believe and learn to find passion in all that you do.

Your Mission

Always seek out hope. Be true to yourself and know that the future holds something great because you love yourself, and you will make sure that happens. Love is in the moment now, even when the moment isn't going as expected. To have hope is to give up some control yet find power in knowing that things will work out. This type of embrace will make it much easier to accept change.

Seek and Celebrate Love

Now is the time to find love in everything that you do. This starts with the mundane. As we mentioned in the last chapter, you can find love in pretty much anything that you do, whether it's a simple part of nature or a small act of kindness. There is love in everything. Seek love within all that you do, from the moment you wake up to the moment you go to bed. Think about when you get ready in the morning; you're loving yourself by taking care of yourself through showers, brushing your teeth, doing your hair, and picking out clothes you like to wear.

Seek love by choosing to do things that make you happy and that will also make you care for yourself. Self-care is essential on the road to self-love. That means choosing foods that are nutritious for you, getting an adequate amount of sleep every night, and getting exercise into your routine to make sure that you stay physically fit. It's not about appearance. It's not about looking a certain way. It's about feeling good about yourself and making good decisions for everything in your life.

Be in love with your job, work on your strengths, and play to them. How can you use your strengths in your job? This is important because it reminds us to follow our passions and seek a career path that we actually like and enjoy. Even if you can't work in a career field that you're extremely passionate about, you can still find love within the thing that you do. How can you use this to help you practice and grow your strengths? For example, maybe you're passionate about singing. One day, you want to be a musician, and you love it more than anything. However, right now, singing isn't really paying the bills, so you have to take a job at a local office working as an assistant. You're seeking love by taking care of yourself. You're working hard to actually have a job that pays good money and makes sure your bills are taken care of, so now you have extra time and freedom to practice your singing career when you're not at work.

Look for these little connections and seek the love in the small things that you do because that will remind you that you're already practicing self-love, thus reinforcing the idea that self-love already exists within you. To love something or someone is a choice we can uphold, and you can choose to flourish that love, or you can choose to neglect it and let it die. Seeking love is a decision. Find love in everything you do. After that, celebrate love, expand on it, share it, and let it grow. Be appreciative that you are capable of self-love and that you are taking the steps to practice it healthily.

Use Small Moments to Empower You

Even when you are unhappy, keep the ball rolling on self-development. Use the smallest moments to empower you. This is why it's essential to take your tasks and break them down into small, manageable parts.

When you have to get 10 things done in one day, break each of those 10 things down into two or more steps. You might think to yourself, *Why would I want to make my to-do list longer?* That's because making things easier to manage gives you more time to celebrate each task! When you complete the first half of a task, celebrate and reward yourself. Remind yourself that you're taking steps to love yourself and you're doing what you need to do to feel good about yourself. For example, if you have to wash the dishes, you might start by first rinsing the food off. The second and third steps would be to fill up the sink with soapy water and wash the dishes. Then, you have to rinse and dry them, and lastly, put the dishes away. All in all, the dishes may be one of your tasks for the day, but if you break it down step-by-step, you can trick yourself into feeling more accomplished since you got more tasks done.

When you finish multiple tasks off of your to-do list, that means that you celebrate multiple times, making it that much easier to keep going and push forward. No matter how hard things may seem on the road ahead, even when you're unhappy, you can still find one small light, and if you take steps to help that light shine, eventually, positivity will spread, and it becomes easier to feel good and happy at the moment.

Search for your true calling and then grow your skill set. Remember that it's the journey, and not necessarily the destination, that matters most. You don't have to have the perfect job in your ultimate dream position to be happy. You can learn how to be happy with what you already have around you by appreciating each of those small moments that empower you. This mindset will help strengthen you while you work on growing your skill set and practice patience on the road to getting what you want. All it takes is one positive choice to inspire two more, which will inspire two more, and then two more until you are only making good choices for yourself.

Think of it like a tree. You are the stump. You are the solid foundation for growth. Now, let love branch off into a few different directions. From there, love will keep growing and growing off these branches, spreading into different areas. This kind of love will help carry you and make you feel good about yourself. Find empowerment in your ability to not only practice self-love but to celebrate these small moments. When you can look in the mirror and feel good about what you see and think to yourself, *I worked hard for that,* it will be the most empowering thing that you'll ever experience. Acknowledge the good things that you've already done in the past, no matter how big or small, because that will keep you consistently working toward growth since you're provided with valid proof and evidence that you're capable of amazing things.

Get Back Up

Don't throw in the towel too quickly. There's no such thing as failure—even the worst-case scenario can help provide us with a more valuable truth. If you learn a lesson and determine what you can do to avoid failure next time, then you are never truly failing.

Don't Be Afraid of Mistakes

Embracing the mistakes that we made in the past was one essential step on the road to self-healing, but now we have to look at the future and not be afraid to make mistakes in the days ahead. Not only do you have to reduce your fear of making mistakes, but it's time to actually seek out opportunities, knowing that you're going to fail and you're going to make mistakes. You're going to mess up, and you're going to have to make up for these blunders. Don't be afraid of making these small blunders because that is how you will learn and grow. The idea of overnight success is not real. What you don't see is all the effort that goes in behind the scenes that an individual has to do to make things happen in their life. No one becomes a billionaire overnight. No one becomes a celebrity overnight. You might not hear of them or see their growth, but that doesn't mean they're not doing things behind the scenes, working hard. They're making mistakes. They're doing things they wish they didn't have to do, but they're doing what they can to find that success.

Sometimes, our biggest mistakes are so much more valuable than learning lessons from others. What can you do to become less afraid of making mistakes? First, forget the idea of perfection. It doesn't exist. Nobody's perfect. Anybody who seems perfect has something going on behind the scenes that you don't know about.

Don't beat yourself up after a mistake. What if somebody else made the exact same mistake that you did? Talk to yourself in the way that you would want to talk to them and help empower them and uplift them because this is the way that you will be able to empower yourself.

Stay true to yourself, and remember that rejection is normal. For every success somebody has, there are hundreds of failures that somebody else has. Life is not a competition. It's a cycle of growth. It's a learning circle, so don't be afraid of feedback. People giving you feedback aren't trying to hurt you or harm you. That's their job. That's their role, and that's what they need to do on *their* path. Listen to others, and don't be afraid to take that feedback because if you are, it's simply your ego blocking the opportunity to change and grow. Think of all of the people who continue to make the same mistakes. What do you think is causing their inability to take accountability, accept that they are imperfect, and make the essential steps needed to grow and change? Don't be like these individuals. Recognize your imperfections, and don't be afraid to be yourself.

Show off your imperfections! Don't be afraid of them! When you share your imperfections with other people, not only do you normalize them and make them less scary to have to deal with, but other people might also give you feedback. For example, if you share with somebody, "I feel like I'm not very confident. I wish I had what it took to be a more outgoing person," somebody might tell you, "What are you talking about? You are outgoing. You are confident."

That can give you the boost you need to recognize that you're being too hard on yourself. Alternatively, maybe they give you some good advice. Perhaps they tell you that you should be yourself and let other people see the side of you that you often hide! As soon as you learn to embrace mistakes and stop being so afraid of them, it becomes much easier to make room for self-love.

Make Sacrifices for Long-Term Achievements

If you want to change and evolve, you're going to have to deal with some pain, but that's okay because you're strong enough to make it through! Anyone that tells you you're not strong enough is not valid. You are capable of making choices that will help support you on the journey of self-love. Humans tend to seek instant gratification, and our modern society only makes that even easier. Instant gratification is a natural human instinct because we have a tendency to preserve our energy. It's important to seek out things that make us feel good. This was a relevant characteristic to have thousands of years ago when we were living off the land and had to depend on the wild. In the wild, you would want to seek out food immediately to make sure that you get resources as soon as possible. It wasn't until we started modern civilization that people began taking resources like food and water and saving it for later. In the past, we simply ate and drank when we could, got sleep when we could, and sought instant gratification. Instant gratification in modern times looks much different. That means scrolling on your phone when you should be working or eating a sweet candy treat when you are bored and not even hungry.

It's important that as we walk down the path of self-love, we seek less instant gratification and favor more long-term achievements. This ensures that we focus on growth and long-term change. Think of it like a house. Would you rather live in a house that was built overnight, or would you rather live in one that took a year to slowly build? Time and effort were put into laying the cement, building the house brick by brick, and adding small, intricate details throughout the house to make it more special and unique. A house put up quickly might not last as long. Good things take time. Think of it like a can of chili you heat up on the stove versus one you spend all day making and letting cook together in a crock pot.

Instant gratification gives us instant results, but they don't last as long. Seek out the things that take a little bit longer because those are the most special things that we can achieve. Instant gratification also keeps us looking for the next good thing, never satisfied with what we already have. Long-term gratification helps us slowly appreciate what's around us. We build anticipation for the good things that are coming ahead. When those good things actually arrive, we learn to appreciate them even more. Think about credit cards for purchases you don't need or overindulging in pricey, unhealthy takeout meals because you didn't feel like cooking. Making quick, impulsive choices like these will keep you chasing after feelings but never actually happy with what you have around you. It's okay to indulge in instant gratification once in a while; you deserve to treat yourself, so don't feel bad if you have credit cards or indulge in fast food or takeouts from time to time. However, if you get too caught up in instant gratification, then ultimately, you fail to flex your patience muscles, thus making it harder to appreciate and wait for good things.

In Summary

There's no shortage of unhappiness in life. We will always be able to find things that can validate our misery and make it seem as though we don't have good things to look forward to. That's where hope can come in to help. Use hope as a reminder that you *will* get there. You will have what it takes to practice and celebrate self-love.

- Your mission is to fight past the negative and don't use that as a reason to turn your back on the path toward happiness.

- Seek out love; don't wait for it to come to you, and celebrate the moments that it does find its way into your life.

- Use the small, mundane, and hidden moments in life to help inspire you to keep pushing when the going gets tough.

- When bad things happen or you get knocked off your path, keep going, pushing forward, and moving to the next great thing.

- Mistakes are a natural part of life, so learn to not only embrace them but seek them out so that you can learn from them in the process.

- Know that true happiness will take time to cultivate, so seek out long-term gratification in favor of things that give you quick but short-lasting results.

Hope is the key that will unlock your happiness, which has been trapped inside a cage of misery, so turn the key and let happiness fill your life.

Chapter 9:

Practice Self-Care for

Your Whole Body

One poll showed the shocking revelation that the average person in the US only felt relaxed for 40 minutes a day at the most (Melore, 2022). Between work and life demands, there's little room for the average person to ensure all their needs are met and that they're taking care of themselves.

But when we fail to care for something, we fail to show it love. When it comes to others, whether that's a close friend or our family, we might go out of our way to show them love. We ask how they're doing, make plans to spend time together, and overall, want them to know that we love them dearly. For some reason, we struggle to give ourselves that same attention.

Be in alignment with yourself and treat your body with respect. Pay adequate attention to your body and how it feels. Your body is a powerful vessel that carries and translates your love and light.

Your Priority

Your health and well-being are the most important things to take care of. If you don't take care of yourself, you surely won't be able to take care of other people. If you don't take care of yourself, you will never feel good about yourself and who you are, leading to even more failings at self-care.

Visualize What's Ahead

On your path to self-love, there are a few things that you'll need, and some tools that can make the process much easier for cultivating a life where you love yourself. One important tool is visualization. Visualize yourself and really picture your future. This doesn't mean just having an idea in the back of your mind about what you hope for the future. Take a minute to close your eyes and really think about what you want in the days ahead.

What does that look like in all aspects? What do you look like? What job do you have? Where are you living? Who are you with? Do you have a family? What kind of friends do you have? How much money do you have? What kinds of things do you eat? How do you like to spend your time?

Visualize your future ahead so that you have a clear picture of what you are working toward. Visualization becomes easier to practice when we take the practical steps for goal setting. Don't just chase after what you hope to achieve mentally; turn it into something more practical that you can physically see.

To do this, start by writing down a list of your goals. There are no rules to what this list can contain. Simply sit down and start writing out all the things that you hope to gain in the future. This can be something small, like buying a new purse. It could be something big, like getting a degree in a career field. Write all of these goals down, and don't hesitate too much as you're writing to help keep these ideas flowing.

After you have your goals written down, go back through and circle the three that are the absolute most important to you right now. What actually has to get done? It's perfectly fine if you want to, in the future, be a successful musician, but right now, your three top priorities might be to get a new apartment, find a stable job, and go to your doctor to get a health checkup. Sometimes, our top priorities at the moment might not perfectly align, or sometimes, our top goals in the moment might not be that overarching dream we have, but they still align with our path toward that goal.

Personal goals that help us will always relate back to our main goals. You have to go to the doctor and make sure your health is in check so that you're mentally and physically capable of fulfilling all the other objectives you need to achieve your dream of being a singer. You need to have a stable house and income to give you stress relief and time to really focus on yourself and your goals. Once you have your three goals written down, then on a new piece of paper, write down the step-by-step process of what it takes to get there. For something like finding an apartment, these steps would be practical things, such as conducting your search online. Maybe there's even a realtor who can help you find a place to live. Ask friends if anybody's moving out or if they know anybody who has an apartment that will be available soon. Finding a new, stable job would start with updating your resume and reaching out to references to see if you can use them on your cover letter. If you need to make a doctor's appointment, this would mean checking your insurance and seeing what doctors are available in your network. Write down all these steps and objectives because that is how you turn your dreams into something more feasible. Once you have all those step-by-step processes written down, you can then start visualizing each of those steps, making your dreams seem more realistic and achievable. Visualization is a powerful practice that will help you gain all the things that you want in the future.

Affirm Yourself and Your Needs

Affirmations are a crucial part of getting what you need in the days ahead. Remind yourself what it is that you are working toward. Remind yourself that you are deserving of gaining these things as well. When you make a choice to take care of yourself, let go of the guilt surrounding that decision. You are worthy of being taken care of. Prioritizing your own needs and setting boundaries is exactly what you're supposed to be doing. It can feel wrong at first because you're so used to hating yourself. You become naturally aligned with neglecting your own needs, so as you realign in a new way, it's going to be uncomfortable. It's like getting a new pair of shoes. At first, they might not be that comfortable, but with time, and as you acclimate, it becomes much easier to feel like this is a normal part of your everyday life. Keep upholding care for yourself, and eventually, you will find what you need to feel fulfilled. Affirm your own needs and boundaries. Remember to use positive affirmations, such as:

- I am capable.

- I am deserving.

- I am powerful.

- I am great.

- I am amazing.

- I can do this.

- I will achieve.

- I will succeed.

- I am loved.

- I am unique.

- I am creative.

- I am worthy.

These are your priorities. Self-care isn't just about taking a shower or going on a trip to a spa. Self-care means being kind to yourself and using compassion internally.

When your day is busy and you feel overwhelmed with the tasks you have to do, it might be easy to tell yourself, *I don't need to work out later*, or *I can just stay up late and only get a few hours of sleep tonight*, because you prioritize work and you think you need to get that done first. However, if you're always prioritizing work, then you're not going to get adequate sleep, and you're not giving yourself the healthy lifestyle you need to feel supported. Eventually, your work is going to start suffering, as well as your mental health, and everything falls apart.

Once you start prioritizing self-care, you'll notice that you become more efficient, you're happier in your relationships, and you're more productive with any work or other endeavors that you have to do. The more that you affirm your own needs, prioritize yourself, and make sure that you're taking the necessary steps to get these things done, the easier it becomes to actually accomplish all of those goals you set and practice the visualization that is going to help you get there.

The Body as a Temple

Treat your body as a temple. It is the vessel that holds all your thoughts and emotions. It is used to connect with others. It keeps you safe and has a complex internal system that helps you recognize your thoughts, needs, and feelings. Give it the love it deserves, and it will reward you in return.

Take Good Care

Do good things for you, like training your brain through meditation or exercise for endorphins and good health. Meditation is the process of slowing down the mind, calming the body, and regulating the mind–body connection. If your mind is feeling chaotic and stressed out, then your body is going to feel that same way as well. That's why it's crucial to slow down and breathe to practice meditation. Start first by regulating your breathing. Take deep breaths in through your nose and slowly let it out through your mouth. You can also start counting to help regulate this meditation. That might mean counting up from one to five as you breathe in and then counting down from five to one as you breathe out. Alternatively, you can count from 1 to 10 as you breathe in and out. Whatever works best for you is what you should go with. Don't force yourself to breathe too fast or too slow, as this could cause a different layer of stress.

Then, as thoughts start to pass through your mind, let them slowly fade away. Don't get stuck to one thought at a time; let them fizzle out just as each breath you take does.

Try to meditate for at least 10 minutes at a time. Then, as you practice more and keep meditating, you'll be able to go for longer periods. Meditation helps pause and soothe your thoughts, making it easier to have emotional control.

Exercise is also a great way to help release endorphins in your mind and maintain good physical health. Focus on your natural human instincts and abilities to help these flourish. Sometimes, when we think of exercise, we picture a gym and drinking protein shakes or having the perfect sets of gym wear—that's not the case. Start simply by walking. Go for a walk for 15 minutes every day. Consider something like climbing, jumping, swimming, or dancing. These are all very natural human types of physical endurance. These activate multiple parts of your brain and help regulate your nervous system, all while providing your body with good physical health. It's also important to keep resting your body through meditative and deep breathing practices, as these help keep you grounded.

Exercise is important, but resting our bodies is also just as essential for ensuring that we have positive health.

There are four core elements of your health that all connect to create a perfect structure for maintaining a happy mind and a healthy body. These include stress management, physical movement, proper nutrition, and adequate sleep. If any one of these four parts of your health is struggling, then the rest of them won't be able to function either. Think of it like a car. A car needs four wheels to drive properly. If one wheel is missing or you have a flat tire, the car could still move, but only so far until the rest of the tires start to get messed up. If you're not getting enough sleep, then it's going to be hard to exercise and make good decisions about your nutrition, and that's going to make your mental health suffer as well. If your mental health is suffering, you might not keep up with exercise routines, or you might fail to follow through with meal plans. If you're not cooking good food for yourself and you're making poor nutritional choices, then it might be hard to get good sleep and maintain positive mental health.

There are many things we can do that can alter the mind-body connection, which is why it's so essential to take good care of yourself. Self-love is all about taking good care. If you truly love somebody, you are going to do whatever it takes to make sure that they are taken care of. You wouldn't neglect their needs. If you truly loved somebody, you wouldn't disrupt their sleep. You wouldn't harm their nutrition. You would make sure that they are taking care of themselves and doing whatever you can to fill in the blanks in their self-care routine because you love them and you want what's best for them. Self-love is founded on this same philosophy.

Make Space for You

Beyond meeting our basic human needs, such as sleep and nutritional requirements, we also have to think about how we deserve a space where we feel safe and happy. That means creating a good home and a place that you can escape to and feel happy inside. That means scheduling time just for yourself for everything you love in life and making some sort of dedication or practice to uphold that.

Date yourself, go out, and do things that are fun, and relish in the time that you are home alone because this will help you not only repair the relationship you have with yourself but it will also help you build a stronger bond and connection. Doing that will make it easier for you to continue to make good choices for your mindset. Your body is a temple, and at times, you've likely hated this body. You wish that it changed faster. You wish that it looked different. You wish that you felt different. You wish you had more energy to do the things that you wanted. You wish you had more intelligence to make better choices for yourself. You wish you had better impulse control to stop self-sabotage, and after a while, you can start to resent your body, but it's the only one that you're ever going to have. It's the only one that is going to support you through this entire lifetime. That's why it's essential to make space for you.

Think about your actual physical space as well. This means maintaining a clean and healthy environment. It means choosing paint colors, floor plans, and furniture layouts that you feel comfortable in. It means choosing the right lighting that creates a warm and welcoming environment and including good things in the space that make you happy. You also need to have space for yourself. You might not be able to have that because maybe you share a one-bedroom apartment with multiple people, or perhaps you even share a bedroom with a sibling. It can be difficult to find space for yourself, but creating a safe environment where you can escape could mean having a nice corner of your bedroom where you can read a book with headphones in and feel like you're in your own world.

Maybe there's a spot in the backyard where you can put a nice chair and plant a small garden so that you have somewhere to go. When you need some alone time, make space for yourself because that's another form of self-love. If somebody came to you and said, "I need space. I don't feel safe here," you would find the space for them to feel comfortable. That's what you'd need to do for yourself because this will continue to uplift you and remind you that you are worth it.

In Summary

The kindest thing you can do for yourself is to practice self-care. Sometimes self-care feels selfish, but it's the exact thing we need to become the best version of ourselves possible.

- Remember that self-care is your priority. Only you can provide the care to yourself that you need to thrive.

- Practice visualization to help you see what's ahead, giving validity to your dreams and making them feel more realistic.

- Affirm yourself and turn down the volume on the negative voice that keeps you held back.

- Treat your body with respect and kindness by showing it love through positive self-care practices.

- Balance your mental health, physical well-being, nutritional intake, and sleep patterns to make you feel more whole and complete.

- Create a sanctuary and have a place where you feel safe and wholesome to help you truly thrive.

As you start implementing small changes into your life and welcome self-care, you will discover a new perspective that helps you see just how harmful you've been to yourself in the past.

Chapter 10:

Plan "You" Time and Time

With Others

How much time do you spend wishing you did something versus actually doing those things? All day long, it's easy to come up with various things we think would be fun or that we'd like to try, but actually doing those things is different. Sometimes, things don't happen because we don't *make* them happen. From dream vacations to simply dining at a new restaurant, it's up to us to decide what we want to do and then actually make plans to do those things.

You've likely been in a conversation with others where one person says, "We should get together soon!" and the other person agrees, yet those plans never happen. Showing love requires that we have initiative. We must take action instead of waiting for others around us to do so.

Make time, and don't delay what you truly desire. Plan ahead and take some "you" time. Make time for others. Take emotion and put it into action to open yourself up to receive all the beauty that awaits you.

Your Routine

The best way to stay proactive is to make plans and then take action to set those plans into motion. Routines help us stay consistent. When you know exactly what you want to do and what you are going to do, it fills in the blanks for decisions that could otherwise cause us stress and chaos. There are a few important elements to keep in mind when building a routine.

Have Fun

As someone who struggles with self-love, it might become normal for you to see fun as something that's simply a reward. You might not go out of your way to make sure that you're doing things that you enjoy and that you actually have fun doing. On your journey of building more self-love, plan regular days of fun and identify what fun means to you in the first place. Don't think of fun in somebody else's context because the things we enjoy are different for everybody. Some people think it's fun to play sports. Other people think it's fun to play video games. Hobbies like woodworking, repurposing furniture, or making miniatures can all be activities that people think are fun. Do you think it's fun to go to museums or the movie theater? For some people, fun is simply sitting on the couch watching a good TV show. Not everybody gets the opportunity to do that, so being able to relax and enjoy your environment might be a simple way for you to have fun.

Pick out the things you love, do them, and then forget about the rest. There are always going to be things in this life that we have to do that we don't want to do, like pay the bills or go to our jobs. Sometimes, we have to work to make money, even if we might not be completely happy with our jobs. The goal, however, should be to do the things you want to do the most and make time to do just that.

Remember that doing things that are fun is not solely a reward—you deserve to have fun no matter what your situation is and not just if you meet certain conditions. You deserve to have alone nights and "me" time. You deserve to say no to certain obligations so that you can make sure time is carved out in your schedule to have fun. That means if you were planning a really fun weekend home alone, doing nothing but your hobby, and somebody asks you to hang out, it's okay to say "no" to them. You don't have to feel guilty, and you don't have to lie or make excuses. You can simply tell them, "I can't this weekend. I'm busy, but thanks for asking!"

Anybody who pushes you or makes you feel guilty about setting boundaries and spending time doing the things you love isn't somebody worth having in your life. They should understand that you also deserve alone time and need an opportunity to decompress and be happy.

Stop spending so much time doing things that you don't even care about. Of course, we all have to work to make money, even when we might not be passionate about our jobs. It is good to push yourself to socialize, sometimes even if you might not feel like it, to maintain connections with other people. However, what's important is to stop doing the things that we don't necessarily *need* to do simply because of the pressures that have been placed on us by society. You don't need to go to every party that you've ever been invited to. It's okay to take breaks sometimes! Carve out time in your schedule for what makes you happy and fills you with joy, and focus on that.

Make Time for Others

You might be wondering, *How do I strike a balance between saying no to certain obligations and still maintaining a healthy social life?* There is a balance at play that we have to keep in mind. You should be able to turn down invitations every once in a while so that you can focus on yourself, but at the same time, you can't completely isolate. Sometimes, we don't like to be around others, or we may struggle with social anxiety due to feelings of insecurity. If you are somebody who struggles to socialize and feels easily burnt out after social events, that's okay. It's normal and common to feel that way, especially if you're struggling with self-love. We do have to remember, however, that social connections are very important, and we *do* need to make an effort to carve out time for others to maintain those connections.

We also have to remember that relationships are a two-way street. Somebody might invite you out and do things, but you also have to make an effort to invite people to do things as well. That way, if you plan to make time for others, you can have more control over when you socialize in your life. If you never make plans to hang out with anybody, and people stop asking you to hang out, you might start to get offended. You wonder what's wrong with you or question why they might not want to invite you. However, they might simply feel that you don't want to hang out with them because you are not making the same effort. That's why it can be very helpful to be the one who plans events, hangouts, and social gatherings so that not only do you show others that you care about socializing and you want to spend time with them, but you also have some more control over your schedule.

Make time for family, whether this is your chosen or biological family. We don't have to be friends with somebody just because we're blood-related, especially if we don't get along. However, create a family that makes you feel good about yourself. These should be close friends, siblings, cousins, parents, aunts, uncles, co-workers, neighbors, and anybody else that you actually enjoy being around. The people who are around you influence and inspire you, and they also offer solace and sanctity from the chaotic world that we all are doing our best to survive in.

Choose to be around people who make you feel whole and prioritize spending time with them. Not all social gatherings have to be big. Pick out a movie and invite a few friends over to watch the movie with you. You also don't have to spend hours and hours with somebody. Give them a call on the phone and have an hour-long conversation on your next day off. Then you can still have the rest of your night to do whatever you'd like! Invite somebody out to dinner or just for a few drinks. You don't have to have a party every time that you hang out with somebody; a simple check-in and conversation can be enough to help two people feel connected. If you are somebody who struggles with socialization, one important tool that can help you feel more comfortable is to ask people questions. Ask them questions about themselves, their lives, and the things that they do. Ask them what movies they're watching or if they've been cooking any good food lately. Ask when their next trip is or how their family members are doing. It's not always easy to socialize with others, especially when we hate ourselves. We get focused on ourselves and wonder if people are judging us or if they think we're weird. As you learn to love yourself more, you'll find that socialization is much easier. You'll see that other people are likely struggling with themselves and the love they have for themselves just as much as you are.

Have Good Habits

Learn the art of being and doing. Everything we do can be considered a habit. How you get ready in the morning, the methods you use to approach work, and the thoughts that influence you are all habitual and may be influenced by your experiences. Notice when you have bad habits and are doing things that may be holding you back, and swap them for better habits.

Add Things Daily

Change is hard because we think that change has to be dramatic. Big changes in our lives might look like a move, a new relationship, or a new haircut. In reality, change happens in small doses. Consider the last time you saw a picture of yourself when you were young. Chances are you didn't realize just how much you've aged because you see the gradual changes of aging in the mirror every single day. Of course, every once in a while, we notice new wrinkles or gray hair, but for the most part, we don't really see just how much we're changing over time until we make comparisons to the past. Then, all of a sudden, we see these drastic changes, but we weren't there for each little moment that our bodies changed. The best and most long-lasting change occurs in very small doses.

Having good habits is likely a goal that you have, whether that means saving your money better and making good financial choices or eating less junk food and more whole nutritious meals. You can decide what daily habits to start implementing in your life.

Recall the list of goals that you wrote in a previous chapter. What are some habits that you can put in place to help make these goals more feasible? As you start creating habits, break them down into small pieces. Let's think of an example. Perhaps you spend a lot of money on fast food. Cooking is just not something that interests you, and it's so much easier to just spend $20 here and there on picking up takeout rather than cooking meals at home. However, you've noticed that this is not only impacting your wallet but also your physical health. You're tired, you're struggling with brain frog, and maybe it's difficult for you to follow an exercise routine because of these physical symptoms. You might have a goal to simply eat healthier. That's a great goal to have in mind. But it's not necessarily a habit. A habit would be the small, intricate steps that we can take to get there. A habit in this situation might be to avoid a certain fast food restaurant. Maybe you tell yourself that you're not going to eat from the local burger joint for a month. Instead, you are going to try cooking new meals. Another habit might be to follow some chefs on social media so you can start learning how to cook different meals. Another habit might be to start saving a few hundred dollars every month for a grocery budget so that you can meal prep. A habit might be to swap out your nightly candy bar with yogurt with fruit. Whatever it may be, pick small habits to add to your daily life.

If you tell yourself, *Starting tomorrow, I'm going to eat healthy*, that's a good goal but not a great plan. It can be very overwhelming to actually take the steps to live a more nutritious life. That's why, instead, we should add one small habit to our life each day. When you make these big goals but have no plans, it's hard to reach those goals because you haven't thought through the steps to get there. Then, when you fail to reach that goal, you might hate yourself, blaming your inherent qualities rather than the lack of plan as a reason for failure.

Make small changes and little choices that lead to bigger results. One day, you might start going on 10-minute walks after a meal. Another day, you might make kale chips in place of potato chips as a healthier alternative. There are so many powerful things that you can do daily that can be easily added to your routine. These include things like daily walks, reading 50 pages a day, decluttering closets and junk drawers, buying a cookbook for healthier recipes, making homemade versions of fast food meals, or getting a standing desk instead of one where you sit so that you're encouraged to move more.

Get creative and think of things that could seamlessly fit into your schedule. It doesn't matter what habits you want to add to your life. The key here is to remember to add things daily and in small doses so that they can build into bigger and better habits over time.

Communicating Effectively

Remember that how we communicate is also a habit. Some people have a habit of talking too much, and others have a habit of not talking enough. Some people aren't afraid to be blunt and say what's on their mind, whereas others will stuff their emotions deep down and never share what's actually on their mind. If you learn how to communicate effectively, it can change everything. Communication isn't something that just happens with others either; it's also how we communicate with ourselves. Learn how you're communicating with your body, and remember to practice the art of saying no. For example, if you start implementing one of those habits into your daily life, then the next day, when it comes time to go on that 15-minute walk, you might tell yourself, *I'm too tired. I'll just start tomorrow.* However, communicate with yourself, have a conversation, and dig deep into *why* you want to push this off.

If you're generally genuinely hurting or sick and you really don't think you can go for a walk, then that's okay, but you have to communicate that with yourself and discuss these things deeply.

As you start repairing your habits around communication, you'll notice that this also impacts your relationships with other people. Reflect on some of the communication habits that you have with those in your life. Do you withdraw from others? Do you talk over others? Do you withhold what you actually want to say? Notice these habits because they could be influencing how other people view you and treat you, which could also be impacting your ability to love yourself. For example, maybe you're a very closed-off and anxious person. You don't really like talking that much, and you're not one who tends to share your emotions with other people. For this reason, maybe you don't speak up that often, and you keep things to yourself. Other people might see this, and instead of recognizing that you're closed off, maybe they think that you don't like them. Maybe you seem annoyed, or they're afraid to talk to you because you're not as willing to open up.

If you notice these things about yourself, then it can become much easier to start implementing small changes. We are all humans, and we all have our own unique ways of sharing the things that are on our minds, so now it's up to you to raise awareness over communication styles to see how that may be impacting your life. Once you do that, it then becomes easier to open your world up to better and stronger habits.

In Summary

Find the balance between making sure you have fun and creating habits that help you thrive. Keep these key steps in mind:

- Establish a strong routine that helps you stay on top of your game, and plan ahead so you can always prepare for your next move.

- Know what fun means in your life, and make plans to ensure that you are able to find fun in small ways.

- Socialize and practice talking to other people to help build your skills and strengthen your ability to form and maintain connections.

- Implement small habits into your schedule daily to help support a healthier lifestyle.

- Don't rush progress; be patient and notice small ways you can tweak habits for the better.

- Remember that communication is habitual, so raise awareness over your strengths and work on your weaknesses in the process.

All in all, establish an important routine surrounding doing things that you love and doing things that are good for you, as this will help you establish routines around self-love.

Chapter 11:

Exist in the Present Moment

At any given moment, your brain could potentially process up to 11 million bits of information (Ramirez, 2020). Consciously, however, we're only aware of and processing around 40 to 50 bits.

Still, this astonishing amount is a reminder of how much work our brains put into the present moment. All around you are little signs and signals that are communicating different things to your body. When struggling with self-doubt, it's easy to ignore everything around us and instead get lost in our thoughts, whether we're dealing with anxiety or fear. Now, it's time to turn to the present moment and fully embrace your experiences. Get out of your head and into the present. Move with each moment rather than staying stuck in the same place.

Be kind and watch the world change with your attitude. Live like there is no tomorrow and you can change the world. Use every moment as one to fully embrace the present as it passes.

Your Gift

Now is the only time we have. The "present" moment is a gift we've been given. Exist in this present moment, and embrace all the amazing things you've been given so far. Sure, there is plenty that you likely still want, but learning how to be appreciative of the world around us is a superpower that will help you through even the toughest times.

Embrace the Present

Embrace the present and let it strengthen you to prepare for what is to come. Right now, take a deep breath in. Now, let a deep breath fall out.

There's no going back in time. We still have to deal with some of the problems in our past, but the good news is that you are not the person that you were in the past. Let go of everything. There's nothing right now that you need to worry about fixing from the past. There are only things to take care of in the present moment. Shift your way of thinking and recontextualize these tasks to help you shed the emotional attachment to things of the past.

For example, consider someone who has excessive debt built up. It can be hard to move on from this and get a fresh start because the debt is a constant reminder of mistakes from the past. However, rather than feel guilt and regret over this debt, this person has to simply accept that now, the responsibility is to simply make payments. There's nothing else that can be done, and getting stuck in regret and guilt only adds stress. Instead, it's crucial to focus on the "now" and do whatever is needed to stay on top of this financial burden. The more guilt that is felt isn't going to mean there's more control over making changes from the past.

Regret only makes us feel worse. It doesn't help us go back in time. It's not our key to switching to a different life. The best thing we can do to make up for the past is to embrace the present moment as it stands in front of us now.

Now, as you move forward, only focus on what you want to build in the future. Know that you've done a great job learning and growing thus far, and remind yourself that you are now going to use that same power to work through anything that is going to come your way. Use this time as a reminder that every little thing you've done and experienced in life has led to this exact moment. There is so much beauty to be found within that realization.

Sure, maybe you lived through difficult experiences, but if you had not, you might not have been able to have the good experiences that you've gained. Sure, things might have been different had you made certain choices, but you made your decisions already, and there's no going back. Now, all we can do is hope that one day, things will pan out. We can work toward amazing things and build toward awesome goals that ultimately make every negative thing we've experienced worth it in the end.

This is an especially true realization for us when it comes to appreciating the people we have in our lives. For example, had you not lived through certain things in your life, maybe you wouldn't have the spouse or partner that you have now. Maybe things would have been different and you would never have crossed paths had you not endured certain hardships. Maybe you wouldn't have the exact children that you have if things went a little differently. One split second can change the course of our lives. If one split second had been different, then your entire life might be different. Now, this is an important realization that can help us find comfort in the present moment, even if it's a moment that we're not quite happy with.

In addition, if you are struggling and you've been through seemingly more negative experiences than positive experiences, then your story could still be a part of somebody else's. You might have had struggles, but maybe all those sacrifices were worth it if it meant that your child was going to have an amazing future. Maybe those sacrifices were worth it if it meant that you saved a friend or helped out a family member. Every small moment you have survived is one that writes your story. Our stories are made up of thousands and thousands of words and intricate details, and if one word was different, then that story might be different. Learn to embrace everything that has happened so that you can fully immerse yourself in the present moment and live the life that you deserve to live.

Always Be Kind

There's a lot in this life that is hard to attain, whether that's financial success, happy relationships, or a strong education. There are many things that we have to work for. One thing that is always free and always available is kindness. Kindness is a small choice that we can make every day, even when somebody is hurting us or being mean. You can still choose to be kind to them. You can see that they're hurt, and the bad things they're doing to you are a result of the negative experiences they've been through that have led them to be the person they are. Even when somebody has done something wrong to you or done nothing to deserve it, you can still give them kindness because it's free and you have an unlimited supply. It might not feel that way. Sometimes, we live through experiences and meet very negative people who make us feel like we don't have any kindness left to give. But that's not the case. You'll always have kindness to give to yourself and to give to others.

It costs nothing to be kind, and the benefits will always outweigh the effort that you have to put into being kind. Even when others aren't kind back, you can still move forward and have a happy life by being kind to yourself and remembering that their negativity doesn't have to define your existence. Remember that those who struggle to be kind may have simply not endured the same amazing things that you have, and they are not on the same path to enlightenment. They haven't powered through and found their own inner strength to lift them out of the hardships that they've existed through. Be kind and hope for the best for them. Wish that they learn how to heal and then move on with their life.

Find peace in this kindness, knowing that no matter what happens, you're always making the right decision and doing what is best in that situation to get you out of it. Kindness will always be the best choice.

Of course, there are extreme circumstances where we don't have to be kind. If somebody is physically assaulting you or emotionally abusing you, you don't have to be kind and giving to them, but these are extreme circumstances that are special outliers. When people are offending you, that doesn't mean that using kindness is a sign that what they did is okay. Instead, it's the acknowledgment that you can still live a happy life in spite of what they did.

If you are in an emotionally abusive relationship with your spouse, of course, your priority in that situation would be to get to safety and be kind to yourself and know that you don't deserve that.

On an everyday basis, however, kindness is readily available. Is your neighbor being rude because you didn't take your trash cans inside quickly enough? Smile and show them kindness. Was the cashier at the store especially rude? Smile and tell them to have a wonderful day. Is one of your friends being passive-aggressive or trying to constantly one-up you in a conversation? Be kind to them, smile, and walk away from the situation to let them see they aren't getting to you.

Being constantly kind isn't about being a pushover or letting people mistreat you. Instead, it's the acknowledgment that other people aren't hurting you as a personal attack but instead as a result of their own unresolved issues. Focus on yourself and remember that you don't deserve mistreatment. You don't deserve to feel a certain way, and those who might be making you feel bad about yourself are living in their own misery. Someone else's misery is not your issue, and it's not something to let control your life. Embrace kindness to help you maximize each moment that you live through.

Shape the World

Spark the passion to want to change the world and then see how that changes you. Instead of seeing the world as yours, see yourself as part of the world. Know your influence and seek the way that you can make positive changes.

Strive to be a Gamechanger

The history of humans and civilization is all dependent on those who were willing to take a risk and be a game changer. Think about all the amazing rights you have today and all the protections that are in place to help preserve those rights. Those were a result of people who were brave enough to go against the grain and take a risk to be different from what they were taught. They questioned what they were led to believe, and they took a stand against that. Forget the traditions that don't work for you and ask the questions that others are too afraid to ask. Even if you find that your beliefs still align after you start asking questions, that's okay. That just means that your beliefs have been strengthened. For example, think of a religion in your life. If you start questioning some of those religious beliefs, you might get pushback from certain people; they'll tell you not to ask certain things, or they might even reprimand you for questioning your faith. However, asking those questions could make your faith stronger. It can help you find deeper reasons and logic to help support those theories and beliefs. If not, then it's proof that maybe those beliefs aren't something you should be depending your life on anyway. This can help empower you, strengthening your relationship with yourself in the process.

Question rules. Maybe you find that a rule *should* be in place, and there is an important reason why it's there, but you still have to learn the art of questioning to help you build your logic and reason. This will strengthen critical thinking and make you more likely to let go of beliefs that end up harming you. If you are a game changer and you're willing to step outside your comfort zone, this is also something that people will admire. It strengthens your ability to be confident because you also recognize that you have so much power. You'll feel good about yourself when you make choices that lead you to question your surroundings and the things that you've been taught to believe because it helps you gain a new perspective on the world.

The chaos of the world can be very overwhelming and overpowering at times. There are so many things outside our control and certain things that we will never be able to change. Conflict happening across the world or secret abuse hidden in a household that we don't see can all be things that make us feel so powerless. We wish we could change and we wish we could make things better. We wish we could feed all of the hungry, and we wish that we could help all of the hurting. But unfortunately, we can't.

However, we do have a very far reach. We can make a small decision that might influence three people. If those three people are then inspired by us, and each inspires three more people, then the chain continues, and that power and influence spreads far and wide. That's the kind of impact that we need to focus on. Don't let yourself feel defeated or powerless because of these huge issues; focus on yourself and your world and be a game changer who can spread that love and power throughout your community, your family, your friends, and even just your household. There's no telling what influence you can have on this world, so don't be afraid to stand up for yourself and what you believe in and let the magic happen.

Move Effortlessly Into the Future

Move effortlessly into the future, and prepare for the days ahead and all that will come along with that. Rather than getting stuck in the past and lingering on things you can't change, make the most of what time you have left. Those who are struggling with self-love might find that it's difficult to move on because of all the things they wish they could change. They wish they could go back and make a better decision for their future. They wish they could go back in time and enjoy their youth more or start saving money earlier. Unfortunately, we can't go back in time and change these things, but what we can do is see ourselves in the present as a past version of our future selves. That may sound confusing, so let's think of an example.

Let's say you're 35 years old. You didn't get a good degree in a field that's very lucrative, and now you're struggling to find a job. You think back on yourself at 18 and wish you had known better. You were ignorant of the world, and you pursued a degree that is in a dying career field. Now, you have to change your life's direction, but you're comparing yourself to your peers, feeling like it's too late for you.

You're desperately trying to survive each day, making quick and impulsive decisions to try and alleviate some of that constant guilt and regret you have over the past. You hate that 18-year-old version of yourself because you were so blind to what it truly meant to build a successful future. Now, years are passing, and you feel like your youth is slipping away from you, and it's too late to make a positive change. Instead of hating that 18-year-old version of yourself, flip the script and love the 50-year-old version of yourself.

See your current self as a past version of what this 50-year-old will look back on. When you're 50, and you're looking back on yourself when you were 35, you'll see just how young you truly are. You'll see how much time you have left and how much potential there is to change. You can either keep living in guilt and regret, hating yourself, or you can make the choices now that you wish you would have in the past.

When you compare yourself to a teenager as somebody in adulthood, then, of course, it's going to be hard to avoid any feeling of regret. However, see yourself as a young version of the future, and you'll start to realize just how much time and change you have left. You can choose a different career field and get a new degree. You could start a business. You could pursue a passion and strengthen your artistic abilities.

No matter what you choose to do, remember that you should focus on loving the future you rather than hating the past you. Accept that we are all humans and move on from the rest. Forgive yourself before it's too late. Rather than wishing you had more time, make the most of the time that you already have. Rather than trying to change things you can't change, take your life in the direction that you're meant to go in. This will empower you to live your best life as the best version of yourself. Change your perspective and become friends with the past, present, and future versions of yourself so that you can build the best future possible.

In Summary

We might not always like our life, but in reality, it is a gift that others would appreciate having. Aging can be stressful, but it's a privilege that many won't get to experience. Embrace the present moment and make the most out of each day by:

- Fully experience each moment as it happens to allow more self-love into your life.

- Let go of the past, as there is no changing or controlling what has already happened.

- Use kindness whenever possible—remember, it's free!

- You might not be able to change the world forever, but you can change *your* world, and that's sure to have a far reach.

- Don't be afraid to take risks and be a game-changer, as this is how some of the most amazing things have emerged in this world.

- Make movements into the future and shift perspectives to help you focus on loving yourself now and always rather than hating yourself from the past.

You have a special power right now to look at the world around you and see it freshly with gratitude. Seize this life-altering opportunity and embrace the present!

Chapter 12:

Get Over Old Gripes

There's no telling how long we'll live, but we can be certain that we are only on this planet for so long. Most people die with some form of regret, but after interviewing caregivers of the dying, it was found that many people share similar regrets.

One of the biggest ones was that most people wished they had let themselves be happier (Warren, 2012). Anger, resentment, rage, and jealousy often occur because someone else did something. However, when we hold onto those emotions, we are the only ones left suffering.

Don't let emotions hold you back. Get unstuck from the past and live for now. Keep moving forward, even when the past is trying to follow you, as you will eventually break free.

Your Burden

One of the hardest things we have to face is that we cannot change the past. There is no time machine or clock that we can turn back and do things differently with. We have to embrace the fact that this is the life we have. The sooner we do that, the easier it will be to move on because failing to embrace the rigidity of time will leave you exhausted and living in resistance.

The Past Is Written

We've talked a lot about how it's important to get over the past and let go of old gripes because there's no changing the past. It's already written, so we have to learn how to live for now.

115

Don't deny the past or stifle the emotions you have. When you recall memories, don't make yourself feel bad for still having regret and guilt from time to time; it's important not to let that regret or guilt lead you to make impulsive or poor decisions but instead, focus on trying to simply alleviate those feelings.

It's still okay to have regrets and wish that things were different. That's a natural part of life, and that's to be expected. That's because it's so much easier to tell what we should have done after the fact now that we know how things turned out.

For example, if you play the lottery, you're trying to pick numbers that you hope will win, and after the numbers are revealed, of course, you say to yourself, I *should have picked that number. I knew that that was going to get called.* In reality, there's no way you could have predicted the future, so try to avoid telling yourself that you should have done this or you should have done that. You can't make yourself feel guilty that the past version of you couldn't predict the future!

Trying to change the past is useless because the past is already written. If you don't move on from the past, you will always be making decisions focused on trying to make up for the past and all the other regrets you feel, which leads to wasting even more time.

It's normal if you struggle with rumination as reflection is a part of our mindset. Have you ever had a memory pop into your head randomly that haunts you, and you can't help but think about it over and over again? Maybe it's an embarrassing memory or a choice you wish you hadn't made.

This is our attempt at gaining control over the situation that makes us feel powerless. The past is written, so it's time to let go of the idea that we need to hang on to grudges.

People change just like you do, which means that maybe they have the same regrets that you do. Maybe they wish they could go back in time and make things different. Maybe they feel insincere because you know deep down that they made a bad decision that hurt you. However, sometimes, our choices impact people more than we ever could have imagined when we were making that decision. It doesn't make you a pushover or weak to forgive somebody and move on. What matters most is that you hold them accountable. Don't let them repeat that behavior and hurt you again. If they do ultimately repeat that behavior, then that's a sign that they haven't taken accountability, and you need to move on.

The past is written, not just in pen, but in stone. Trying to change what is written could end up breaking the whole stone apart, so embrace what is already there in permanence and move on to live life anew.

Enjoy This Destination

Discover the art of being happy with where you ended up. Sometimes, it can be difficult to enjoy the destination because of jealousy, but don't get stuck in that trap—you don't know what others have been through in their own stories. Somebody might have had an amazing first half of their life, but maybe the second half won't be so pretty. For example, perhaps you feel like you're behind in your age group. Maybe you haven't gotten married yet, and everyone around you is starting families and having children. Maybe you're still simply trying to figure out what you want to do with your life, and you don't know what career path to take. You feel like you're behind and like you need to rush to catch up to where everybody else is.

Who's to say that their life doesn't go downhill? Maybe they get everything they want. They have a family, a house, and kids, but maybe their spouse ends up cheating on them, and it all falls apart. Perhaps their children have some struggles in school, and that consumes their lives, making it difficult for them to focus on their own dreams and passions. Perhaps they get lost in this life and realize it's not something they wanted, and they'd rather have the freedom you've been given. Comparison will always rob us of the joy that we have in our lives because everybody's story is different. That's what makes us so beautiful and so unique. It's because we each have our individual paths that we've gone down. If you're always trying to take detours to follow somebody else's path, then you're never going to be happy because you will get lost on the road and fail to make it to your destination.

You'll struggle to embrace the world around you, and there will always be something new that you can use against yourself to make you feel inadequate. You'll always be able to find excuses that leave you feeling as though you're not good enough. Stay grounded in reality and remember that no one is perfect. In fact, sometimes, the more somebody tries to come off as perfect, the more flaws they're trying to hide.

Their perceived perfection is your projection.

You're not looking at the flaws when you think somebody's perfect; you're simply focusing on all the good things they have. Social media can exacerbate this perceived perfect identity, leaving you feeling constantly inadequate. As you learn to love yourself, the good and the bad, it becomes easier to embrace this destination that you've wound up at and be happy for the unique path that you've been given.

Let Go of Past Definitions

Don't let the past define you. Sometimes, there's a pressure that we hold onto to keep up with the past. If we keep making the same mistakes, we might never have to admit they're mistakes.

Give yourself permission to move on from the past and remind yourself it is not a defining feature of who you are. Sometimes, we might have trouble letting go of the things that aren't good for us because of the fear that the past was a waste of time. However, learn from the past and embrace what you've been through. Show yourself love to build the courage to move on.

Make the Most of What's Left

Enjoy the ride of life. Make the most of what's left. Maybe some things have happened in your life that have broken you down, and it seems like there's no piecing it back together. However, take those broken pieces and make a beautiful mosaic. Grind up those broken pieces into sand and mix them with a plant's soil to help it grow. These are just metaphors for how we can take the pieces of our lives, no matter how small or broken or shattered, and create something beautiful and amazing from which we can grow.

Make the decision right now to let go of the small stuff and focus on the bigger picture. Be the bigger person and show respect for others, even if they disrespect you. Spend your day doing what you want to do, and take each moment as an opportunity to learn and grow. Holding on to grudges is only going to weigh you down and hurt you more than anyone else. Your resentment of another person doesn't impact them, but it does impact how you make decisions and move throughout your day.

Remember to keep practicing breathing exercises. Breathe in a new life—one that's renewed and rejuvenated and focused on happiness, and feel yourself shedding the past, letting go of the things that cling to you and making you feel like you're stagnant in the present as you breathe out.

Seek out new experiences and enjoy the things that you already have. Find fun and excitement within the mundane and share those experiences with other people. Look for the positive in the situation. When you find yourself focusing on regret or wishing you had done something differently, focus on what you did or said that was good because, chances are, that's what people are truly remembering; others aren't as focused on your flaws as you are.

Don't Get Stuck on the Future Either

It's crucial to think ahead and plan for the future, but at the same time, don't get stuck in the future.

Don't spend all your time tethered to the days ahead because that could be an alternative way that you're neglecting yourself in the present. Yes, it's important to be responsible and make long-term decisions that will set you up in the days ahead, but not at the expense of enjoying the present because it's not about the destination; it's about the journey. Slow down and enjoy that journey. Enjoy that ride because it will make the actual destination that much more exciting once you finally get there.

Many people get caught up in chasing their future, which leads them to rush through things like marriages or welcoming new children to the family. Some people feel rushed to find the perfect career, so they take career paths that they don't feel fully fulfilled by because they feel the urge to get their life started now.

When we put too much pressure on the future, real situations around us are less exciting. Enjoy each moment for more peace and clarity, and don't put pressure on time that isn't right now in this moment. Make good decisions now that will help you naturally lay the foundation for the future, but don't get so caught up in it that you lose sight of what's around you.

What's one regret you have from the past? Chances are, you wish you would have appreciated your past more. Think back to the days when you were a kid and you didn't have anything to worry about but getting your schoolwork done. Think about being a teenager and all the exciting things that came along with gaining freedom and exploring new things. Consider how, as a kid, teen, or young adult, you could eat whatever you wanted and get little sleep or take poor care of your body because youth helped you power through.

Chances are, you feel regretful that you didn't appreciate this more. Right now in this moment, you're never going to be younger than you already are, so learn to appreciate that moment because, in the future, you're going to regret not enjoying your life. Sure, you may end up at a good destination, and you may have everything you ever wanted, but if you don't have those fun experiences and memories to support you, then that destination might not be as exciting either. Living in the present means balancing our regrets of the past and our hopes for the future and actually enjoying what we are experiencing with each moment. You deserve to have rest. You deserve to feel good about yourself, and you deserve to be happy, so embrace each moment and rejoice in the present because that is how you will repair the relationship you have with yourself and learn to love yourself on a deeper level.

In Summary

Whether you have old gripes with others or yourself, let these go, as they do nothing but harm you and hold you back. Let yourself enjoy the present and future by moving on and starting fresh.

- No matter what we think, say, do, or feel, we will never, *ever* be able to change the past.

- The past is already written, but that doesn't have to be a bad thing; this unique story is simply the backstory to our biggest successes.

- Enjoy the entire journey, as well as the destination that you've wound up in because it is a journey that is uniquely yours.

- Shed the definitions that have confined you in the past and write the rest of your story with more power.

- Make the most of what you have in the days ahead as an act of endless self-love.

- While the future is important, don't speed in the other direction as you let go of the past and get fixated on making the perfect future.

Life is a ride; learn to enjoy those ups and downs rather than fearing them.

Chapter 13:

Build Real Relationships by

Loving Yourself

Out of the 8 billion people to exist on the planet, research shows we are likely to meet 80,000 of them *at the most* (Roser, 2023).

The thing about all of these people is that no two are alike. Yet, despite our unique characteristics, many of us still manage to find people who we like and who like us back. Whether you are in a relationship, have multiple friendships, or are close with your family, you know the magic and beauty that can be found in the connections you have with other people.

Unfortunately, however, relationships can also bring our lives stress, chaos, and endless conflict. When we fail to love ourselves, it could mean ending up in relationships with people who don't truly love us either.

Love yourself to love others better. When you understand how to show yourself unconditional love, not only do you reinforce important boundaries, but you also secure stronger relationships by identifying what you deserve.

Your Influence

When you learn to show your love to yourself, it becomes easier to give love to others. By loving yourself, not only do you help you, but you help those around you. See the power of self-love as a force to improve relationships.

As primates, we've learned to gather intuition for centuries, which helps us make judgments about others just by viewing them in social settings (Ludden, 2016). This means that when others can see you love yourself and that you're exuding this love, you become stronger.

One theory to keep in mind is the practice of nonattachment theory. This is a focus on finding a balance between our emotions, relationships, and material possessions as a means to help manage the influences in our lives. The nonattachment theory emphasizes finding harmony between letting go of the need for control and making the most of our life's experiences. Let's take a look at a few ways this can be done.

Love Is a Magnet

You will attract the kind of love that you give to yourself and raise awareness over what you attach yourself to in this world. Are you dependent on a good relationship for happiness? Are you dependent on getting material things or showing off these material possessions to other people? Are you dependent on your emotional state to determine your outlook on life? You will attract the kind of love that you give to yourself, so that means if you become the partner or the friend that you want, then you will attract the kinds of partners and friends that you deserve.

Be the hard worker that you would want to work with. Be the spouse, girlfriend, or boyfriend that you want to have in your life. Become this version of who you are meant to be, and let love exude from you. Focus on yourself and what's happening inside rather than the external. Focus on doing your best for the joy of being the best version of yourself rather than the actual outcome, whether that means material possessions, wealth, or acknowledgment from peers and family members. Pursue your personal growth without being fixated on what outcomes are coming your way, and grow because that's what is ethically, morally, and justifiably right to get in your life.

Nonattachment theory emphasizes finding peace, clarity, and happiness within your life, and we can only do that once we let go of the things we've been attaching ourselves to. Instead of attaching yourself to these external forces, learn how to become dependent on yourself by focusing on authentic love and tapping into who you are at the core.

This helps you learn how to surround yourself with the people and things you deserve. Others will become attracted to this version of you, almost like your love is a magnet, pulling them in and filling your life with even more peace and happiness. You're giving up all your power when you attach yourself to external circumstances like an individual's love for you or a material possession you want to gain. To be the person you want to be, continue to practice letting go of material possessions and other things in your life that you've been caught up chasing so that you can start the process of being the version of yourself you're meant to become.

Putting Together the Puzzle

Love is like a puzzle. We have to put all the pieces together to help us see the bigger picture. For example, one puzzle piece might be activities and hobbies you do that you love, such as artistic endeavors or sports you're enthusiastic about. Other puzzle pieces are forms of self-care, like brushing your teeth in the morning and picking out clothes that make you feel good about yourself. Once you start to put all these pieces together, you'll see the bigger picture: that you are lovable, deserving of love, and capable of giving that love to yourself. Keep organizing these puzzle pieces and search within yourself for the answers to the questions that you often find yourself asking. Each piece of the love puzzle represents a different component that is deep within yourself, like trust, passion, and values for any relationship, whether that's one that you have with yourself or one that you have with another individual.

These pieces all need to come together to help you create a harmonious picture of a life filled with love. Self-love is your foundation for better relationships. If you don't love yourself, then you're not going to find yourself in good relationships. You're going to end up with partners that you don't deserve and who hurt you, and you're not going to make changes because you don't believe that you deserve any better. If you have self-love, then you know that when someone's treating you poorly, you have the right to stand up for yourself and make a change so that they can't continue to hurt you anymore. In any puzzle, sometimes pieces become missing, and you can still see the picture, but it's not a whole and fulfilled puzzle piece.

That is where self-love can come in and help fill in those blank spaces. You can identify what you need and what you're missing. You can identify what hurt you with that puzzle piece, and you can solve the mystery of where this puzzle piece went missing. You can make gaps between the puzzle pieces and fill those in with more forms of self-love that will help support you on your journey. When it comes to a puzzle, all pieces also need to fit together. If two pieces aren't fitting together, then maybe that's a sign that something in your life isn't working or is preventing you from fulfilling that puzzle piece.

In a puzzle, sometimes some pieces seem like they should fit into space but ultimately don't match up. Self-love gives you that awareness to think clearly and figure out how to put all the pieces of your life back together so that you are capable of fulfilling your destiny and creating that image of what it means to love yourself wholly.

Know Good Relationships From Bad

Mind games don't exist in a real relationship. Acknowledge the red flags of relationships. Sometimes, we get stuck in toxic relationships because we don't think we deserve better, or we don't even realize that we are treated poorly in the first place because we are so used to such treatment. Real relationships are built on loving yourself, knowing your worth, and accepting what type of behavior you deserve.

What You Seek

Building a good relationship with yourself is the important first step, but now it's time to recognize what you seek and how that may be damaging you. Relationships are things that come into our lives that could either hurt or harm us. The wrong relationship can be incredibly destructive, and the right relationship can be a complete savior. This goes for both romantic relationships and platonic relationships, as well as even relationships you have with people you work with. The type of relationship you seek may be unhealthy, and you could be getting into it unconsciously, not aware of just how much you are self-sabotaging yourself.

Sometimes, we fall into bad relationships because we don't have the self-esteem to see that we deserve more. We believe that we're getting the best relationship that we can have. In addition, we might have experienced bad relationships in the past, so we have a skewed perspective of what it means to actually have a loving and wholesome relationship. When it comes to relationship expectations, there are a few things to keep in mind.

First and foremost, you deserve to have your needs met. If anybody tells you that you're undeserving of love, finding fulfillment, or following your passions, then they are not good for you. If you are with somebody who's not willing to make sacrifices or go out of their way to make you happy, then they are also not good for you. Reflect on any ways that you might be self-sabotaging with your relationship. Are you drawn to a certain type of person who isn't necessarily good for you? Do you tend to suffer from insecurity that keeps you from speaking up or getting what you deserve? Sometimes, we are afraid to make changes in our relationships or stand up for ourselves because we become dependent on that relationship. We hate ourselves so much that we aren't comfortable being alone, and we believe that being alone is worse than being in an abusive or emotionally destructive relationship. Some of us are so fearful of ourselves and what it means to practice self-love that we would rather continue to live in a world of self-hatred because it has become so normalized in our lives.

You shouldn't be afraid of your partner when they come home from work; you should be excited to see them. When you're spending time with them, you should enjoy each moment. You shouldn't stifle parts of yourself to make them happy. It's okay to get slightly annoyed with a partner every once in a while. When you spend so much time with another individual, that's bound to happen. Conflict can arise, especially when two people have strong opinions. However, generally, the relationship should be 90% good. You might go through a rough patch, but it should be just a moment in your relationship, not something that defines the entire connection.

Explore your relationships and dive into yourself to reflect on how your motivations lead you to certain types of relationships. Are you trying to seek fulfillment from a relationship? Are you using this as a form of dependency for your self-worth? If this is the case for you, you're placing your emotions on outside circumstances and attaching your happiness to things that are outside of your control.

Relationships should not be things in your life that are dependent on whether or not you're going to be happy. You should be able to be happy on your own and find fulfillment within yourself.

Relationships can assist us, support us, and make things easier, but they shouldn't be the resolutions to the deep problems within us because then we'll never actually solve those problems. When the relationship goes sour, or that person is no longer in our life, then all of the problems that we have been ignoring for so long come back even harder that we have to deal with. Deep down, we may know this, which is why we end up getting stuck in bad relationships.

So you must stand up for yourself. Know what's right and be brave enough to admit when a relationship is wrong or when you might be seeking out a negative relationship.

Learn Your Language

What steps can we take to manage relationships? This involves learning your language. All of us have different kinds of language that we use to communicate our emotions, feelings, and thoughts. Some people are very outgoing, and they express their emotions right away. Other people have to sit and reflect on how they're feeling to help formulate understanding within the words they choose to use.

Some individuals completely stifle their emotions and stuff down all these feelings, never sharing them or expressing them with other people. Learn how to be a careful communicator. This means first identifying how you feel, processing that internally, and then sharing that with other people. How do you express love? How do you receive love? Knowing this will help you better understand your relationship and how they've been impacting your life. When you're in the middle of a conflict, take a moment to think about what's happening. Why are you hurt? Why is there conflict? What is the deep core issue that's happening here? Once you identify that, you can then start to process your emotions and feelings. How is this impacting not just your mind but also your body? Do you feel yourself stuck in a fight or flight mode where it's hard for you to respond to the other person and interact with them in a healthy way that supports both of you?

Are other people triggering you and making it hard for you to stand up for yourself? Do they tell you things that make you want to internalize what they're saying? Is it hard for you to process what's happening? Do you find it difficult to share what's on your mind with this other person? Reflecting on all these things will help you learn your love language so that you can strengthen your relationships in the process. That's why self-love is so important. It's because that's our first relationship to prioritize. The relationship that we have with ourselves can be improved and be a form of practice for us to know how to set boundaries, say what's on our mind, and express how we're feeling effectively. Once you're able to love yourself and establish a relationship that you've worked hard to build in your own life, you'll then be able to share those things with the people around you.

In Summary

To love others in the best way possible, learn how to first love yourself. Know what it means to forget expectations and instead embrace your unique qualities. Reducing these judgments will help you learn how to go easier on yourself as well.

- Don't let external things influence you; focus on your core values, as these are what mean the most.

- The love you put into the world is the love that you will receive back.

- Love is a puzzle, and figuring it out will help you see all of the unique ways that you can show love to yourself.

- Differentiate relationships that are good for you and those that keep you from loving yourself.

- Recognize what you knowingly and unknowingly are seeking out to gain a better sense of how you show love to yourself.

- Identify how you share and communicate with others to strengthen your language and improve relationships.

The strongest relationships form when we learn how to love ourselves.

Chapter 14:

Learn to Fuel Connections or

Know to Let Go

Can you think of someone you know who is in a bad relationship? Maybe their marriage is falling apart, or perhaps one of their friends keeps mistreating them. Despite the clear indication that things aren't working out for them, do they find it difficult to have the strength to leave?

To others outside of this relationship, it may be clear that things need to end. But for this person, perhaps they don't see anything wrong with their bond, or maybe they are simply too afraid to leave.

Now, reflect on your relationships. Chances are, someone you know is thinking the same thing about your connections that you might be thinking about others. It can be hard to let go of old relationships, especially ones that have been around for a while. However, there's a powerful difference between a good relationship that needs a little work and a relationship that is better off ending—and knowing the difference can be the hardest part.

Your Freedom

Your relationships are your choice. Knowing the difference between what helps and hurts you is a freedom you can grow to help you build the life you want. Relationships originate from you, your partner, and your intimacy. At the end of the day, relationships should be freeing, not restricting. Can you breathe? Do you have space? Do you enjoy being alone more than you do with your partner? These are the types of things to discuss with ourselves to realistically evaluate the impact of a relationship.

Relationship Imperfections

As you start to navigate your relationships, you might be wondering, *How can I tell the difference between a toxic relationship and a relationship that just has a conflict to work through?* The thing to remember is that connection doesn't happen with the snap of a finger. It can be hard enough to love ourselves, so of course, it's natural that it might be difficult to love somebody else. When we meet somebody that we are infatuated with, we tend to focus on the good things about them. This is especially true in the beginning stages of a romantic relationship. It might be easy for you to overlook those red flags because you're so enamored with them and you're so relieved and refreshed by a positive and healthy connection. Disagreeing here and there is fine, and it's something that's to be expected. What's important is to evaluate how someone handles this conflict, the type of conflict that seems to arise, and what happens after that conflict is resolved. How do they interact with others? Do you see patterns in the relationships that they have with other people? What patterns are visible across their relationships? For example, if you meet somebody you get along with and get closer with, you might eventually run into some conflict. As you argue with them and start to have some issues, you might notice that they tend to withdraw and isolate, and they're not very good at expressing their emotions or what they're feeling at any given time. That's okay. Not everybody's able to fully express themselves in the same way. However, if you look at all of their other relationships, you might notice that there are issues there. Maybe they don't have any close family or friends because they've isolated themselves to the point that they cut people out of their lives. That could be a red flag that they're not willing to own up to things and work on issues. If somebody is reserved and withdrawn but tends to have good relationships with people in their life, then maybe they just need a minute to talk about conflict, and maybe they're the type of person who wants to process their emotions before they discuss them with you. This is just one example of how we can raise awareness over patterns we see in others to help us assess whether we're in a good relationship that needs work or a bad relationship that should end.

As you reflect on the relationships an individual has with others, also look at the relationships that you have and what patterns are across those relationships. Noticing this can help you gauge between what's a healthy relationship and what's not. Do you tend to fall into healthy relationships, or do you find yourself chasing after the exhilarating ups and downs that can sometimes come with toxic relationships? When there is a bond where there is a lot of intense fighting and emotional back and forth, it can be addicting because we feel thrilled from the intense highs that come after the intense lows. Be conscious of this and notice if you have a tendency to choose "roller coaster" relationships. Continue to reflect on this to help you become more aware of yourself.

Pay attention to any type of tendencies you have to self-sabotage or isolate from other people. Look at the pattern of conflict as well. It's okay to have a fight with somebody, share what's on your mind, and express what you need them to do to change. Do you need them to be more expressive? Do you need them to communicate more? Do you need them to listen to you more? Then, when the next conflict arises, look at the differences between this one and the last. Is it the exact same problem as last time? It's okay if the problem happens again as long as you see some improvement. It's going to take some time for them to change.

If, after five issues where the same conflict keeps happening and there is no change, then that's a sign that this is a toxic situation that requires more intense effort. If you find that there have been improvements over time, then that's a good sign. That's a sign that you're strengthening your bond with this person, and both of you are holding each other accountable so that you can grow and actually change for the better.

There isn't always one instance that defines a relationship, but instead a pattern of repetition. You also have to be emotionally willing to be patient and wait for that change to happen, so if you are getting into these conflicts where the other person is especially harmful to you and it's degrading you, then it's okay to move away from that relationship. Even if they are slightly improving, you can tell them that you need

133

more and you're not seeing all of the effort they're putting in. If they aren't willing to make those sacrifices, then chances are they aren't ever going to actually change in a way that is going to protect your health and your peace.

Relationships are imperfect, but they should still be mostly happy. The majority of your conversations should be good, and the majority of your day-to-day life should be positive. If five out of seven days of the week you're fighting and two of those days are good, that's not a good relationship. We can get stuck in these relationships because we start to feel so defeated that those two days feel especially good. They give us hope for the rest of the time that we'll be spending together. But in reality, that's not enough. That's eventually going to break us down, burn us out, and damage the relationship. Long-term relationships should be mostly good, and some conflict is normal, so focus on patterns and change over time to help you determine what you should focus on and what you should let go of.

Know Your Roles

Relationships don't exist just to make us happy; we also have to play a role in somebody else's life and repair and build up the relationship as well. Assume your role is that of a loving partner. It's your duty to make sure that the other person in your partnership is happy and taken care of. Their pain points are not going away, so if you want to make things work, then it's time to listen to them when conflict arises.

You have to change as well. You can't just expect everybody else around you to do the work of all the relationships in your life. You have to cater to you and your needs. You also have to be somebody who's making an effort and showing the other person that you care. Relationships should be mostly 50/50. There will certainly be times when maybe you're struggling, and somebody else needs to step in and take care of you, but then the balance needs to go back to 50/50. Then, when they are struggling, it's your duty to step up and take care of them. If relationships are constantly 80/20, the partner doing 80% of the work is always going to be suffering and may even become resentful. Strike a balance and work together to create a harmonious bond.

Set goals with your partner and support each other on this journey. Work with them, not against them. Relationships aren't competitions. They're partnerships, where two parties want the same thing and are both willing to work toward that and help each other out. Identify the strengths of your relationship and why it's important for you to help work on this relationship because that will turn into the motivating factor for you to keep pushing each other and working to repair your bond.

Relationships will take work and effort, but they shouldn't be so exhausting that you feel drained. The work should feel worth it. It's normal to have a conflict a few times a month, but when it's something that's happening multiple times throughout the week, that's not a good sign. You shouldn't be having that many frequent fights. You shouldn't be having that many frequent conflicts. If so, that means that one of you is not willing to calm down, think things through, and really work on the core issues. When you are bickering all the time, and there are always these little problems happening, it's usually a sign that there's an even bigger issue going on.

If you find this is happening, take the steps to acknowledge the issue and make a plan to address that conflict with your partner. Assume your role as a valuable member of every relationship you are in, and you will discover that you start developing stronger habits.

The Art of Letting Go

Leaving a relationship and letting go is not always easy. The heartbreak of broken relationships is a sting many try to avoid. However, it's important to know how to move on when something is no longer meant for you.

Love yourself and embrace the healing process. Celebrate your status as someone single, or be okay with being comfortable with yourself even if you are in a couple.

Being lonely is not the same as being alone!

Those who love themselves are okay with being alone, and that is an important skill to master to prevent yourself from entering bad relationships just out of loneliness.

Don't Lose Yourself

When we fall into a relationship, it can become easy to lose ourselves. This happens in a partnership. It may even happen in a family relationship. You might lose yourself in your role as a mother or father. You might lose yourself in your role as a son or daughter as you become a caretaker for your parents.

Sometimes, we want the other person to be happy because that makes our lives happy. We want to take care of the people around us because we love them. However, you can't neglect the relationship that you have with yourself for the sake of making sure you're taking care of others. This is especially important in terms of emotionally abusive relationships. People who break us down make us feel as though we are not worthy or that we are not equal to them, thus making us feel like we have to go out of our way to take care of them. Don't stay with the wrong person, as it damages you in the long run, depletes your motivation, and destroys the relationship that you have with yourself as the relationship you have with the other person takes its place.

If you choose to stay with someone, remember to shape and nurture your own identity. It's great if you and your partner get along and love all the same things, but do your best to find things that you still love on your own, whether this is a toxic parent, partner, or friend, and prioritize taking care of your emotions and maintaining healthy boundaries to prevent them from taking over your life. Don't let others break you down in terms of what you like and are passionate about. Not everybody has to like or approve of the things that you do. You don't have to share every hobby or interest with somebody else.

Maintain your identity as an act of self-love. If you loved someone, you would want their personality to shine. You would want to make sure they're supported enough to feel comfortable with themselves. Don't lose yourself in this relationship, and instead, prioritize yourself in all relationships.

Be Okay With Being Alone

Discover the art of being okay with being alone. Being alone might be the biggest fear of somebody who struggles with self-love. If you don't love yourself, then you aren't going to enjoy being alone because you won't be able to hang out with that person. If you were stuck in a room with somebody you disliked, of course, you would be unhappy, so when you don't like yourself, you are not going to be able to live a life of fulfillment. You might feel anxious about all the thoughts you have, or perhaps you're struggling to enjoy things without someone else's approval. Practice loving yourself and embrace the healing process. Know that you are going to continue to be imperfect and that you might never be perfect, but what matters most is the effort you put in and the love you give and share with yourself.

Celebrate your status as someone single or be okay with being comfortable with yourself. Even if you have a partner, you have to learn how to be alone. If your partner is going on a trip or a vacation, or they have to travel for work, then it's important to learn how to love yourself because you need to be able to enjoy that time alone. This is the time when you would want to practice your hobbies and take yourself on dates, like going out to dinner on your own or watching a movie that you love that maybe your partner doesn't like as much.

Being by yourself is okay! Loneliness isn't something that has to happen every time you're alone. In reality, you can still feel lonely even if you're in a room full of people. Learning how to love yourself helps curb loneliness because you'll be able to enjoy each moment, no matter who surrounds you.

It's very easy to start losing ourselves in a relationship, and that's when we begin attaching ourselves to that relationship, thus impacting how we feel. Of course, if a relationship ends, it's going to be difficult, but it shouldn't determine your worth or your life's purpose. Finding your own meaning will help strengthen your relationship because you'll take some of the pressure off that relationship to be perfect. See relationships as something to enhance your life—not define it.

In Summary

Know how to add fire to a relationship and when to call it quits. Learn the art of how to build lasting relationships and when to cut things off.

- You get to decide who you let in your life and who you let go of.

- An imperfect relationship isn't doomed; learning how to work on these imperfections can actually make it stronger.

- Play an active role in relationships and take steps to show the other person that you love and care for them just as they do for you.

- Not all relationships have to last forever; it's okay if you ultimately decide that one should end, as even relationships that are over can still provide meaning in our lives through the memories and lessons we learned.

- Remember to maintain your identity within your relationship to prevent losing yourself or becoming dependent on the other person.

- Learn how to like being alone, and you'll never be lonely again.

The connections we have in our lives can become a source of self-love if we learn how to manage them properly.

Chapter 15:

Break the Chains of Society

One in 20 men and 1 in 20 women "reported being dissatisfied with their appearance" (*Body Image*, n.d.). There's no denying that society places immense pressure on us to think, act, and feel a certain way. These immense pressures contribute to how we view ourselves.

The last part of learning how to love yourself is to let go of feeling pressure to be the version of you that society wants. Remove yourself from the bubble of society's expectations, and you will free up enough space in your life to learn how to truly love yourself.

Your Truth

Listen to yourself and your truth and break the chains of society. Understand the motivations behind why we are forced to conform (money, power, and societal pressures). Understand that your non-conformity is discouraged because it isn't as easily controlled. When you are a part of the masses, you're more likely to be influenced by popular culture and other influences that society creates.

Be your own person and recognize your uniqueness. Remember that when you are struggling with non-conformity and you feel uncomfortable, it's because you've been pressured to feel a certain way for so long. We are taught from a very young age to fit in. Humans are group animals, and we depend on others for validation, support, and, at times, happiness. This is why you might not want to show your truest self; you're afraid of what will happen if others see that version of you. Now, as you enact more forms of self-love, it's time to live your truth. Break the mold you've been put into and let your truest self thrive.

The Molds That We Conform To

Life as any human is stereotyped, and these preconceived notions can destroy our chance at loving ourselves. Society creates a sort of timeline for us to live and makes it seem that we should improve with each age. In reality, life is filled with highs and lows. You might have good periods now and bad periods later in life. This kind of conformity makes it seem like individuality is flawed, and there's something wrong with us if we express that individuality.

Forget what you've been pressured into thinking about yourself for so long. This goes back to your childhood. What's the first thing you were taught to think about yourself? Do you recall the first time insecurity was instilled in you? When did you first realize you might be different from others? Shining a light on these truths will help you practice self-love as you begin to heal from the things that hurt you.

Break free from the mold, and you will realize just how much more comfortable you are. Once you learn how to stop caring what other people think, you'll be shocked to see just how much better you feel.

Breaking Free

Break free from the mold of what society expects. First, look at what your core beliefs and values are. Do these align with society? Why do you think these are different or similar? Next, consider your taste or the things you like. Do these align with society's expectations? How do you express your unique voice in the world around you?

Tap into your roots and talk to your inner child. What opinions did they form about themselves at an early age, and how has this impacted the way that they moved throughout life? Identify this, and you'll see where your insecurities were planted.

Lastly, find your community. You might feel as though you don't fit in with society, but surely, you'll find a community you *do* fit in with. There are people out there like you—you are not alone! When you are able to find this community, it provides an outlet and form of support that will help you feel validated, thus enabling you to love yourself more.

Society's Expectations

Whether you are a man or a woman, the expectations placed on us are harmful. Before we are even born, expectations are placed on us. Boys' nurseries are filled with trucks and masculine things, and girls' rooms are draped in pink. Not all forms of gender identity are bad, but this is one way that we can see just how far back society's expectations for certain genders can be. Let's break each of these expectations into two categories to help you recognize the intense pressure of society.

Society's Ideal Woman

Women can deal with some tough expectations in their life. If you are not delicate, feminine, motherly, and more, you are not seen as a woman. You have to have perfect skin, hair, and style while being sexy but also modest. You must be thin but not too muscular. You must be well-groomed yet still an effortless "cool girl."

There is no winning as a woman, and the expectations are paradoxical. A woman's worth is taught to her at a young age, and sometimes, they are taught that their purpose lies within their ability to care for a man.

These pressures weigh heavily on women and make it easy for a girl to hate herself at a young age as well. If you are a woman or you know women in your life, redefine what it means to be a woman. What beauty standards are placed upon you, and why has this been harmful? Why do you feel pressured to follow these beauty standards? What do you lose out on by not following these standards?

As women, it's important to start reducing the standards that you put on other women. When you let go of these ideas, you make it easier to create space to love yourself and welcome new perspectives. When you judge others less, you judge yourself less because you remove those pressures to be a certain way. Reduce standards for women in the world around you, and you will reduce standards for yourself, thus making it easier to appreciate your unique qualities and love who you are.

Society's Ideal Man

Society can be just as brutal on men. As a man, you must be a protector, breadwinner, and great father. You must be strong, stoic, and rarely emotional. You must be tough and rugged and detest anything too feminine. If you show emotions, you might be chastised and made to feel as though you are not "man" enough. These ideas can be taught at a young age, meaning men neglect their feelings for much of their lives.

The pressures that both men and women feel actively harm each other, causing issues in relationships and self-identity. When men are expected to be masculine but are feminine, they may be looked down upon. When women are expected to be feminine but are masculine, the same things occur.

We have to realize that each gender is just as unique as the individual; there are no specific rules for what it means to be a man or a woman. You don't have to define yourself with the rules that society has created.

As a man, let your emotions free! Know that it's okay if you aren't rugged or what society thinks is "tough." It's okay to enjoy things seen as feminine—it doesn't make you less of a man. It's okay if you don't feel fully connected to the expectations placed upon your gender. What matters most is our strength and ability to love ourselves.

There's nothing wrong with breaking free from the mold. There is only one unique you! Let this person enter the world in their truest form and craft a life that caters to self-love.

In Summary

At the end of the day, we can't change the way society works. We can influence it in ways, but ultimately, we are still impacted by what we already endured. Now, take the necessary steps to break free from the molds that have confined you.

As we close out the last chapter, think back on all the summaries we've discussed so far. What lessons have resonated with you the most? What has helped you start loving yourself more? What do you think you need to work on the most? This type of reflection is crucial for strengthening the relationship you have with yourself.

Self-love is the most valuable tool that you will utilize to heal from the past and get the things you want in the future. You know what it takes to get there, so now it's up to you to implement these strategies into your life.

Conclusion

Are you ready to love yourself? Have you discovered what it is that has been holding you back from showing yourself love thus far? What steps are you going to take to show that love? What are you going to do when you feel self-hatred creeping back in?

Knowing these things will help ensure you are set up for success in the future. Remember not to let the worst doubts of those around you creep into your mindset. Forget the pressures, demands, and hate that others send your way.

The only person's opinions that truly matter are your own. Learning to establish this kind of self-love is one of the most profound experiences you will ever have.

Now, you've been given the necessary skills to love yourself, and it's your mission to start implementing these lessons in your own life for the greater good. You now have the choice to take small steps because you believe in yourself, and you know that you *deserve* to love yourself wholeheartedly.

Show up every day, no matter what the circumstances. Love yourself in good times and in bad times. Thank yourself for your choices and decisions, and remember all the work you've put into giving yourself the compassion you have a right to have!

Accept that you can change the world with small deeds and make someone's day brighter. Don't just love yourself, but love others around you. Soon, you will find that you are an endless fountain of love and compassion. The choice is yours: will you choose to love yourself today, tomorrow, and the days after? There's no telling what lies ahead, but you can be certain you will be there, by your own side, ready to help yourself through the ups and downs.

We only have one life, mind, body, and one ability to love. Use it to show yourself the warmth, kindness, and validation that has been building inside of you, waiting to be unearthed.

References

Allen, S. (2018, May). *The Science of Gratitude*. Greater Good Science Center. https://ggsc.berkeley.edu/images/uploads/GGSC-JTF_White_Paper-Gratitude-FINAL.pdf

Body image in adulthood. (n.d.). Mental Health Foundation. https://www.mentalhealth.org.uk/our-work/research/body-image-how-we-think-and-feel-about-our-bodies/body-image-adulthood

Cherry, K. (2023, October 31). *Ego as the rational part of personality*. Verywell Mind. https://www.verywellmind.com/what-is-the-ego-2795167

Ludden, D. (2016, September 10). *How others see you*. Psychology Today. https://www.psychologytoday.com/us/blog/talking-apes/201609/how-others-see-you

Melore, C. (2022, July 15). *Self-care shortage: Americans feel relaxed for just 40 minutes a day*. Study Finds. https://studyfinds.org/self-care-americans-relaxed-40-minutes/

Palmer, C. (2020, November 1). *Harnessing the power of habits*. American Psychological Association. https://www.apa.org/monitor/2020/11/career-lab-habits

Ramirez, R. (2020, July 15). *Understanding unconscious bias*. NPR. https://www.npr.org/2020/07/14/891140598/understanding-unconscious-bias

Roser, M. (2023, July 27). *The limits of our personal experience and the value of statistics*. Our World in Data. https://ourworldindata.org/limits-personal-experience

Summer, A. (2018, May). *The science of gratitude.* Greater Good Science Center. https://ggsc.berkeley.edu/images/uploads/GGSC-JTF_White_Paper-Gratitude-FINAL.pdf

Summer, J. (2024, May 8). *How long do dreams last?* Sleep Foundation. https://www.sleepfoundation.org/dreams/how-long-do-dreams-last

Warren, B. (2012, July). *The top five regrets of the dying: a life transformed by the dearly departing.* National Library of Medicine. NIH. https://pmc.ncbi.nlm.nih.gov/articles/PMC3377309/

Wells, D. (2017, July 7). *Fun facts about the heart you didn't know.* Healthline. https://www.healthline.com/health/fun-facts-about-the-heart

Printed in Great Britain
by Amazon

61486179R00090